GET
FIT cycling

Dave Smith

A & C Black
London

Thanks to

Carmel for putting up with me while I wrote this book.

Jemimah and Solomon for distracting me while I tried to write this book.
'Computer Mark' for saving my hard disk.
God, for inventing legs, knowing full well that we'd need them one day to ride bikes.

Published in 2005 by A & C Black (Publishers) Ltd
37 Soho Square, London W1D 3QZ
www.acblack.com

First published in 2001 as *Fitness Trainers: Cycling for Fitness*

Copyright © 2005 Dave Smith

ISBN 0 7136 7203 X

A CIP catalogue record for this book is available from the British Library.

Note: Whilst every effort has been made to ensure that the content of this book is as technically accurate and as sound as possible, neither the authors nor the publishers can accept responsibility for any injury or loss sustained as a result of the use of this material.

Cover photograph courtesy © PhotoDisc
Photos on pages iii, 18, 26, 40, 78, 108 © Photo Disc
Photo on page 90 © Comstock
Photos on pages vi, 4 © Digital Vision
Illustrations on pages 67–74 and 82–8 © Jean Ashley
All other illustrations © Dave Saunders

Printed in Singapore by Tien Wah Press (Pte) Ltd

Contents

Preface

Cycling is a sport of equality, available to men, women and children alike. It need not be expensive, and under medical advice and supervision, it need not exclude the elderly, disabled or infirm. On top of this, of course, cycling offers a pleasurable and efficient means of transport.

Many people find cycling an enjoyable means of improving both their fitness and their health without the injury risks associated with 'weight-bearing' activities such as running. Even if you are a complete newcomer to cycling you will experience positive 'training' effects within days of commencing a regular training programme.

The aim of this book is to provide practical and accessible information for both the beginner and the already-practising cyclist – helping you to understand the complete range of benefits offered by the humble bicycle.

Dave Smith

1 Cycling, health and fitness

Why cycle?

Why choose cycling for fitness? One answer is that it offers a highly enjoyable variety of ways of getting fit – from the stationary bike in your local gym or health club, to the relative relaxation of road riding, the challenge and exhilaration of off-road, and the possibility of many different kinds of competitive activity.

Another, equally important, answer is that recreational cycling, like running and swimming, is a highly effective form of aerobic activity which helps to develop greater efficiency of the heart, lungs and circulation (cardio-respiratory system), which in turn leads to improved fitness and health.

> The chief benefit of cycling for an hour and a half every day is knowing that you can eat whatever you like! I'm a sucker for ice-cream.
>
> *Nick, a cyclist for 10 years*

Fitness benefits

It is generally accepted that improvements in fitness levels, achieved through safe and controlled means, can help to protect against ill-health and disease, as well as bringing a wide range of other physical and psychological benefits.

Given the huge growth of the fitness industry over the past 15 years – and the accompanying growth in understanding of the various processes involved in physical exercise – it is perhaps surprising that many people still confuse the notions of being 'fit' and being 'healthy'.

Health may be defined as a person's freedom from illness; whereas fitness refers to the ability of someone to undertake mechanical work, such as lifting and moving objects, efficiently. It is therefore possible to be healthy without being fit, and vice-versa.

Health benefits

When you start to exercise regularly, you will notice improvements in your basic fitness. However, increasing your activity levels can bring a range of additional, health-related benefits, both physical and psychological.

There are a number of illnesses that are known as hypokinetic, which means that they are either caused or aggravated by an inactive lifestyle. Obvious examples are heart disease and obesity.

In terms of physical benefits, regular activity can help:

- reduce the risk of dying prematurely, especially from heart disease
- reduce the risk of developing other diseases such as diabetes and cancer of the colon
- reduce blood pressure in people who already have high blood pressure
- increase metabolic rate, and thus control 'weight' – i.e. reduce body fat
- build and maintain healthy bones, muscles and joints
- boost the immune system, the body's main defence against illness and infection
- improve strength, co-ordination and mobility in older adults

Weight loss

Cycling, an excellent form of aerobic activity, uses up fat as well as carbohydrate, and can help improve the body's efficiency at burning fat, thus losing weight. This 'fat burning effect' is often a key factor motivating an individual's training programme.

Cycling can be the ideal way to aid your weight loss. When you are doing an activity that you enjoy and can easily incorporate into your life, you'll stay motivated longer. Increasing the intensity of your workouts as you become fitter can only help more.

> Cycling to and from work gives me lots of time to think without the distractions of public transport. It can also provide relaxation, a race (against myself and against others), or a challenge — depending on how late I set off, how soon I have to get home, and whether the wind is blowing in the opposite direction.
>
> *Nicholas, a cyclist for 7 years*

Mental benefits

Exercise also has many psychological benefits. It has been shown to increase levels of a chemical found in the brain known as monoamine, a mood controller which acts to increase positive thought. Hence the saying that exercise can be a drug! There is also some evidence that it can raise levels of a group of chemicals called peptides – in particular, those known as opiate peptides – which are thought to contribute to the 'feel good' factor that often accompanies an especially challenging workout.

The generally accepted psychological benefits of regular exercise are as follows:

- increase in self-confidence, emotional stability and independence
- reduction in anger, anxiety, depression, tension and confusion

A regular, sustained exercise programme in general, and cycle-specific training in particular, can bring about huge gains in fitness and health – and therefore in what is often referred to as 'quality of life'. The following pages aim to show that even a complete newcomer to the bicycle can quickly and easily take up this highly enjoyable activity and see improvements over a very short time.

2 Getting started

There are four main forms of cycling available to the fitness enthusiast: road, off-road, indoor and track. Your choice will depend on many factors including where you live, your budget, your adventurousness, and the fitness goals you wish to achieve. This chapter will examine these in turn, seeing what they have to offer in terms of fitness gains and enjoyment, and also exploring them in terms of financial commitment and possible hazards.

Different types of cycling

Before embarking on a fitness training programme, consider carefully which of the options below – or combination of options – is most suitable for you. The likelihood of starting and successfully maintaining an exercise programme will be greatly influenced by the level of enjoyment you gain from your chosen activity. Choose your activity carefully and you are much more likely to embark on a fitness programme that will not only enhance your health, but also give you great pleasure.

Road cycling

This can be recreational or competitive. Recreational cycling doesn't require the structure and planning needed for serious racing or touring. It is seldom necessary to buy specialist lightweight equipment and provided you have a safe and correctly sized bike, regular rides of between 20 and 60 minutes can be enjoyable and improve your fitness.

Riding on roads or on cycle paths is the most popular form of cycling. Given a reasonable level of fitness, the novice cyclist can soon be covering 30–50 km in a training ride. Although increasing traffic volumes pose some safety hazards, even the most congested cities have traffic-free parks, paths and tracks. The speed that can be achieved on a paved road is exhilarating and has led many mature, 'born-again' cyclists back to the freedom of childhood activities. The rural cyclist may have a myriad of small country lanes to explore, and many waterways have adjoining paths which are suitable for cyclists.

At the outset, even if your ultimate aim is road touring or racing, specialist equipment is seldom required. Many top road-racing cyclists started out by riding their mother's shopping bike!

Off-road cycling

The invention of the mountain bike has brought a superb means of improving fitness, with the added challenge of developing the bike control skills necessary for cycling over rough terrain. Despite its name, the mountain bike isn't just a tool for climbing mountains; most people have access to an area of land suitable for off-road, traffic-free cycling, and in many cities there are dedicated recreational areas for this purpose. Many people also use mountain bikes on the road, but while they can be suitable for most off-road and on-road cycling for fitness, road bikes are not suitable for rough terrain (see also pp. 8–10).

Indoor cycling

Whether in the home or at a gym or health club, by cycling on an exercise bike – or ergometer – you can gain a good level of aerobic fitness without venturing outside. Many stationary cycles have electronic monitoring which you can use to set and achieve your performance goals. Although often frowned on by mainstream cyclists, there is no reason why your entire cycling fitness programme cannot be accomplished indoors. Indeed, if you live in a particularly hilly area, a stationary cycle may be a necessary tool for gaining the initial fitness required to conquer the surrounding roads.

Many fitness centres offer indoor group cycling sessions, where members of a group ride while following the directions of an instructor. Recent advances in indoor bike design have made them feel much more like a regular outdoor bike. If you already use the facilities at a fitness club, stationary cycling can provide a stimulus for fitness without many of the costs involved in the more traditional forms of cycling.

Track cycling

Riding on an indoor or outdoor cycle track, or 'velodrome', is seldom a viable option for the fitness enthusiast. The small number of tracks available, the need for specialist equipment and instruction, and the fact that most track sessions are aimed at the competitive cyclist, make track cycling best suited to the more experienced, conditioned athlete.

> Since taking up cycling I have become healthier and less stressed. I feel invigorated!
>
> *Simon, a cyclist for 15 years*

Types of bike

Having chosen a cycling activity, you now have to select a suitable bicycle. There are bikes to suit all tastes, skills, ages, riding terrain and budgets. However, the main thing to bear in mind is that it is not necessary for you to have expensive cycle equipment to follow an effective fitness programme. What is essential is that you have a bicycle which fits you correctly and is in sound mechanical working order, that you are safely equipped and have comfortable clothing. You may have a bicycle in the back of your garage that your mother used to ride. If it is mechanically sound and fits you well, this bicycle is good enough for fitness training – you will get no fitter riding an expensive new bike straight from the cycle shop. When choosing your bike, you will need to decide between one of six main types.

Road bike

Road bikes with 'skinny' tyres (18–30 mm) are still popular for long recreational rides, touring, fitness and racing cycling. The classic racing or competitive riding bike will have larger and much narrower wheels than the mountain bike (see p. 9), and a narrow saddle. A racing road bike may be as light as 8 kg, as opposed to 12 kg for the mountain bike. Almost all new racing road bikes are fitted with 16-speed gearing (see p. 11).

Sport or touring bike

This has wide-range gearing, and is a good choice for riders who need some carrying capacity but do not require the very low gears or tough frame and wheels of a mountain bike. Its drawbacks are a slower ride and less agile handling compared with the more nimble sport and racing bikes. This is because the frame is designed for stability when carrying heavy loads.

The old-style touring or expedition bike, which can carry 50 pounds of camping gear, will have wider tyres – up to 35 mm – and will weigh more than the sport bike, but will be comfortable for all-day rides. The addition of a third chain-ring will provide low gearing for steep ascents with luggage. Most racing bikes and most sport or touring bikes use traditional 'drop' handlebars the width of the rider's shoulders, although tourers tend to use a wider bar which bends less tightly in the drop section.

Mountain bike

A true mountain bike is more durable than a road bike and can take the abuse of rough trails. It has smaller wheels than a road bike (26 inches or 650 c) and a fatter tyre (up to 100 mm wide) with aggressive tread patterns and a greater capacity for holding air. It also has a flat or curved handlebar and a slightly more upright riding position. Its structure enables it to manoeuvre easily on rough terrain, at both fast and slow speeds.

Mountain bikes are usually 2–3 kg heavier than equivalently-priced road bikes, with a frame size 2–4 inches smaller for a given rider. This again allows greater manoeuvrability and reduces the risk of injury from crash impacts on the top tube. Many mountain bikes are now sold with a front suspension system, usually in the form of telescopic forks. Some designs include rear suspension.

Hybrid bike

The hybrid bike is basically a mountain-style bike that has been adapted to work better on pavements and trails. It's lighter and rolls more freely than a mountain bike, but is sturdy enough for some trails. Its wheels are of the same diameter (700 c) as a road bike, but the tyre width is narrower than that of a mountain bike. Its upright riding position is also like that of a mountain bike. A hybrid is probably the bike most suited to recreational riding and general fitness training.

Stationary bike

The correct choice of exercise bike will make the difference between seeing your fitness develop and progress, or having to find room in the attic for another well-intentioned fitness purchase. Most bikes now have some form of integrated computer which allows you to monitor your training. Have a look at a local fitness club and see which stationary bikes they use, and then to spend perhaps the first couple of months of your programme using them. This will tell you whether or not you'd prefer outdoor riding. A good alternative to the stationary bike is to use a 'turbo-trainer' which simply attaches to your normal bike so you can use it indoors.

Track bike

This is the simplest type of bike, with a racing-style frame and size but no gears or brakes. The rear wheel lacks any free-wheel facility, so that when the bike is moving, the rider has to pedal. If you do choose track cycling as your route to fitness, you would be well advised to contact your nearest track to try out their bikes before making a purchase.

How to choose your bike

To decide which of the above types of bike will be most suitable for you, first assess where you want to do most of your riding. Do you want to ride on- or off-road, on a track, along a canal towpath, through a park, or over mountain trails? Then bear the following guidelines in mind:

Type of activity	Type of bike
Open road	Racing, sport-touring
Road/light off-road	Hybrid
Mostly off-road	Mountain
Urban commuting	Mountain/hybrid/road with heavy wheels
Solo riding	Mountain/hybrid
Group or social riding	Racing, sport-touring
Riding with luggage	Sport-touring/hybrid with rack eyelets

Buying your bike

Avoid cheap mail-order or 'super-market' bikes. They may be suitable for a few years of abuse by a growing child, but their unwieldy weight and inferior quality could soon dampen your enthusiasm. Instead, look in established bike shops, where there are high-quality products and skilled personnel to help you to select a bike that fits your body and your needs. They will also be able to undertake any maintenance work your bicycle may require.

Although it may be early days in your cycling career, try to be realistic about how committed a cyclist you are likely to become. If you think cycling may become an increasingly important part of your life, it pays to buy a better bike than your current fitness requires. Then as you progress as a rider, you'll still own a suitable bike.

A good starter bike should have a strong but light frame made of steel alloy or aluminium. Preferably, wheels will have aluminium alloy rims (they're actually stronger than steel and make the bike accelerate, handle, and stop better), as well as sealed or shielded bearings to keep the hubs and pedals turning smoothly without the need for frequent maintenance. Brakes should be strong and not fade or 'bite' too suddenly. The gear-changing system should be foolproof with shift levers that have audible click stops.

A question of gears

Bicycle gears normally consist of different-sized 'cogs', the overall purpose of which is to enable the rider to maintain a constant pedalling speed whether climbing, descending, or cycling on the flat. For the purpose of cycling for fitness, it is sufficient to know that the lower the gear the easier it is to pedal – and conversely, the higher the gear the harder to pedal.

If you're already fit for cycling, you could probably cope with the higher, more closely spaced gears of a road-racing bike. Higher gearing allows you to ride faster, but requires more effort by the muscles, and therefore a higher level of fitness. If you're not that fit, but your goal is to become so, a racing or sport-touring bike is still appropriate if you choose one with a moderate gear range.

If you have no interest in riding hard and fast, and want to pedal as painlessly as possible, the wide range and ultra-low bottom gear of a hybrid, tourer or mountain bike is for you. If you buy a mountain bike, you'll have plenty of low gears; these make pedalling easy in most conditions, and even if you are race fit, you may need them to climb the steep hills typical of off-road riding. The steeper and/or longer the hills that you face, the more you'll appreciate a bike with low gears. Do bear in mind, though, that a cycle shop will be able to change your gears to make steep hills easier should you buy or already own a bike with high gearing.

Fitting your bike

All bicycles used for training and racing should be properly fitted to the rider. An experienced rider can usually fit their own bike; others should go to an established bike shop for advice. Without specialist help, you can roughly assess a frame's suitability by examining the 'crotch clearance'. This is the space between your body and the top tube when you stand flat-footed in front of the saddle. If you know your inside leg measurement, the difference between this and the stand-over height of a bike is the crotch clearance.

The length of the top tube should allow a comfortable riding position with your elbows slightly bent, no matter where you grip the handlebar. Your back should flatten when your hands are in the drops. Don't expect the handlebar stem to make up for too much variance in the top tube length, since either a very long or very short handlebar stem can compromise handling.

Positioning

Correct cycle setup is vital if you are to train successfully. Even experienced cyclists may find that there are points which they have missed, so, while aimed primarily at the novice, this information is important to all cyclists.

There are two common errors. The first is to set the saddle too low. This places a great strain on the knees and the thigh muscles and

Women and 'cycle fit'

Although over 50 per cent of adult bicycle riders are women, most bikes are still designed by, and sized for, men. Women generally have a shorter torso and longer legs than men, so usually a bike built for a man needs a top tube between 1 and 2 cm shorter if it is to be ridden by a woman. Many women are missing out on cycling comfort for want of a few simple and cost-effective adjustments that can bring vast improvement. There are three main ones, relating to the handlebar stem, the brake levers and the saddle.

- A typical, stock handlebar stem forces women to lean further over the frame than men, putting pressure on the front third of the crotch, exactly where it is least wanted. Ask for a shorter stem to be fitted, so that you can keep your elbows bent when you ride. Remember that although a flat back is recommended for racing, it's not ideal for many women riders because of the likelihood of knee to breast contact – as well as increased pressure on the front of the pelvis

- Many women experience an ache in their hands after a long ride. It isn't necessary – brake levers with a shorter reach are the answer, so you don't need to stretch your hands to apply the brakes

- If you bought your bike from an average bike shop, chances are it has a long, thin, flat seat – perfect for men, but completely unsuitable for most women. A saddle should provide support to three areas of bone in the pelvis – one at the front and two at the rear. The female pelvis is wider at the rear, so women should choose a saddle with a wider rear section. Some also have cutouts at the crucial point of contact with the seat, and can greatly reduce discomfort from pressure and friction makes swift progress difficult. The second is to place the heel, rather than the ball of the foot, on the pedal. Eliminating even these two simple mistakes will greatly enhance your efficiency, giving the feeling of sitting 'within' the machinery of a bicycle, rather than simply being perched on top of it.

Saddle position

Assuming that you are riding a bicycle of the correct frame size (see p. 12), the first step is to set the saddle at the correct height. Many adults set their saddle so that when stationary, they can place their foot flat on the ground. Although many of us were taught this as a child, it will not give you an efficient riding position. When cycling you are rarely stationary, so it does not really make sense to compromise efficiency in favour of comfort when stopping and starting.

■ Begin by setting the saddle height to allow full leg extension when the heel is placed on the pedal at the bottom of the pedal stroke. So, when you are seated on the saddle with your leg straight, your heel should just reach the pedal (see opposite). When your foot is correctly placed on the pedal – with the ball of the foot above the pedal axle – your leg will be slightly bent at the knee and you will be in an effective cycling position (see opposite).

■ Slide the saddle on its rails so that the centre of the front knee is directly over the pedal spindle when the cranks are horizontal. This fixes the position of knee, femur and pelvis in proper relation to the bike frame and the cranks (see overleaf).

■ Holding the saddle level, look at it from the side. The broad area of the saddle – and only this area, not the whole saddle – should be perfectly level when you sit on it. Depending on the design of your saddle, it may be necessary to tilt the nose of the saddle up, but no more than 5 degrees. Levelling this broad area prevents you from sliding forwards, planting you firmly on the saddle and cradling you while riding. You may need to re-adjust your seat height slightly to compensate for this angle adjustment (see overleaf).

*At correct saddle height, you should easily be able to reach
the pedal with the heel when the leg is stretched*

*At correct saddle height, your leg should be not quite extended
when the ball of the foot is on the pedal at its lowest point*

A plumb line dropped through the knee should pass through the pedal spindle

Saddle position

Handlebar position

Opinions differ on the height at which the handlebar should be set. However, for the purposes of fitness cycling you should aim for heightened comfort and control with your back at an angle of approximately 45 degrees while your hands are on the highest part of the handlebar (see opposite). This can be achieved by raising the stem and/or rotating the handlebar until the brake-hoods are slightly more upward. Although your position will be slightly less aerodynamic as a result – possibly making riding into the wind unpleasant – you can remedy this by 'crouching' over the bike (bending your arms at the elbows) when necessary. A more upright position will also help you to breathe more easily because your lungs are not as compressed as they would be if you were leaning over. If your bicycle frame is the wrong size for you, it may not be possible to achieve this position.

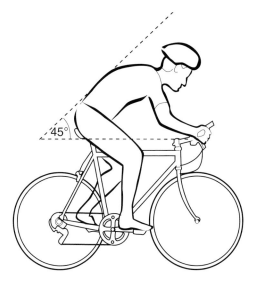

Correct cycling position – back at 45° to tube

Feet position

The ball of your foot should rest on the pedal, immediately over the pedal axle. If you are using cycling shoes with cleats attached to the soles, you will need to adjust the cleats so that when you are clipped into the pedal, your foot will be in this more effective, forward position. It may take some trial and error before you find the perfect setting.

3 Equipment

The advice given in the previous chapter will have helped you choose and fit a suitable bike. However, you still aren't quite ready to ride! There are some items of equipment that you must have for your safety and comfort. Others are optional accessories which can make cycling more enjoyable.

Essential equipment

Cycle helmet

Unfortunately, some cyclists do not regard a helmet as perhaps their most essential purchase. A helmet will protect your head from serious injury in most types of incidents – from impact with an errant driver to an off-road crash onto rocks.

It's easy to protect yourself: modern helmets are generally light, well-ventilated and attractive. However, you will only get maximum protection from your helmet if it fits well – riders with ill-fitting helmets suffer discomfort ride after ride, while the helmet may not really protect them if they crash. In normal riding the fitting pads keep your helmet sitting in place, but the straps are critical when you crash and your head is suddenly and violently jerked about.

Make sure your helmet is the right size; your local cycle dealer should be able to advise you. Also check that your choice meets the recommended ANSI and SNELL safety standards.

Helmets always have at least one set of foam fitting on the inside. Many come with more that can be used to customise the shape. Make your helmet fit with the pads touching your head all the way around, without making it so tight that it will be a constant nuisance.

With the helmet on, fasten the buckle and take a few minutes to figure out the strap configuration and keep fiddling until you get it right. Then adjust the length of the chin-strap so that it is comfortably snug. It should be snug against your chin, with the 'V' of the side straps meeting just below your ear. There should be no slack. When you are done, your helmet should feel solid on your head but comfortable. It should be worn horizontally, not tipped back with the front pointing upwards. You will know if you are wearing a helmet correctly – you should forget that you are wearing it most of the time, just like a seatbelt or an old pair of shoes.

Clothing

For general training, padded Lycra shorts, a moisture-wicking undervest, a short-sleeved cycling shirt, and cycling gloves should allow you to cope with temperatures of between 16–25°C in relative comfort.

Match your clothing to the conditions: nothing can make you more miserable on a long ride than wearing the wrong clothes. The following are some suggestions for a variety of climatic conditions. Whatever you wear, the visibility of your clothing should be a major consideration; bright, reflective clothing is essential for safety when riding in 'hostile' traffic or, for example, on dimly lit country lanes.

Cycling in hot weather

In humid, hot weather, 'wicking' — the transportation of moisture away from your skin to the outside environment — is key. Various synthetic fabrics such as 'Coolmax' permit wicking, keeping you dry (or at least drier) and more comfortable.

In hot, dry weather, your sweat evaporates before it gets a chance to perform its cooling duties. A suitable fabric will therefore be a blend that incorporates cotton for a softer, more comfortable feel and synthetic fibres to enable wicking.

Cycling in cold weather

In cold, dry conditions start with a wicking layer, then add layers of insulating synthetic fabrics such as polyester fleece. Finish with a wind-proof and water-resistant shell layer. Waterproof fabrics – even 'Gore-tex' – do not breathe as well as most lightweight 'water-resist-ant' fabrics and may leave you chilled by the accumulated sweat under your jacket.

No sooner do you hit the trails, then the rain blows in. Be pre-pared. Layer well, but instead of finishing with a lightweight, water-resistant fabric, you'll need a shell that is truly waterproof. Be sure to choose fabrics that 'breathe', otherwise you will create your own rainstorm under your jacket.

Cycle shorts

These are available for touring and racing. Both types have a large piece of material called a chamois. This provides a smooth, absorbent, padded surface between you and the saddle, which reduces chafing. Cyclists generally don't wear anything underneath such shorts, although seamless underpants can reduce discomfort caused by chafing.

Racing-style shorts are made of stretchy, body-hugging fabrics such as Lycra. Such shorts should fit snugly without being restrictive. The more contoured fabric panels, the better the fit (eight panels signify premium quality). All shorts are not created equal, and women in particular should be aware that there is now a growing number of clothing companies which cater for their specific needs, offering a more appropriate cut of material and shape of inner padding. Wash shorts after every ride to prevent rashes and sores.

Gloves or mitts

Cycle gloves are an important piece of safety equipment, because in a fall – when your hands naturally go out to protect your body – their thick, padded palms will prevent cuts and bruises. Gloves also distribute the pressure of the handlebar across your palms, thereby preventing blisters, chafing and nerve compression. You can choose from models with foam, gel, or liquid cushioning. A good fit means no looseness or binding, with tight, even seams that won't unravel. Towelling fabric on the thumb or back provides an absorbent surface to wipe your mouth or nose.

Tools

A small saddlebag, which attaches underneath the saddle, is a good way to store emergency items. However, there's no hard and fast rule about which tools you should carry. It may help to ask yourself three questions.

- How well do I maintain my bike? Poor maintenance means a specific bike failure is more likely to occur.
- Which repairs am I able to make? Unless riding with another more experienced cyclist, there is little point in carrying tools for repairs that you can't carry out.
- How far from civilisation will I be riding? If you only do day rides close to home, flat-tyre tools and coins for the phone may be enough.

Although each bike may require different tools for maintenance and repairs, most modern bikes are standard to the extent that the following will be sufficient for the majority of on-road repairs and adjustments.

Essential tools

- tyre levers
- spare tube
- hand-pump
- patch kit
- adjustable wrench, 6 mm
- screwdrivers (straight and Phillips head, as appropriate)
- hexagonal (Allen) wrenches of 4, 5, and 6 mm

Water bottle and cage

These sometimes come with your bicycle. If not, buy two of each. Regular intake of small amounts of fluid during cycling is essential.

Lights

Battery-powered lights can provide more than adequate vision and safety cover. If most of your training will be done in poor light it may be worth investing in a high-powered, re-chargeable system. Such lights are bright enough to allow full-blown mountain biking at night! Whichever lights you choose, be aware of the battery run-time and carry spare batteries and bulbs. Always use reflective clothing and accessories to increase the chance of being seen by others.

> Commuting by bike keeps me sane. The city never becomes a drag because I'm constantly seeing new things. And if I do get bored, then I just change the route and discover a whole new London all over again.
>
> *Chris, a cyclist for 12 years*

Bicycle lock

If you intend to park your bike in a public place, you will need to secure it. Choose the most expensive lock you can afford, and ensure you lock the bicycle to an immovable object! If your wheels have quick-release levers, remove the wheels and pass the lock through the frame and both wheels.

Optional equipment

Cycle shoes

Trainers have built-in cushioning for shock absorption so if you wear these shoes for cycling, much of your energy output is absorbed by the cushioning before it ever gets to the pedal, which is not efficient for fitness. A bike shoe, however, has a firm sole, so more of your pedalling effort actually propels the bike. Instead of flexing, the shoe remains rigid and the majority of the force generated is transferred to the pedal, thus assisting forward movement.

However, while cycle shoes can make you more 'efficient', their stiff soles make walking difficult. Touring shoes are a good compromise between efficient energy transfer and comfort when walking. Toe-clips, a cage attached to the pedal that you slip your foot into and tighten, go a step further. A clipless pedal system offers the most technological advantage by attaching your foot to the pedal with special pedals and a cleated shoe.

Eyewear

Sports glasses become more popular each year, and with good reason since they offer protection from wind, dust, bugs, grit, glare and ultraviolet light. Look for sports glasses that wrap around the field of vision, permitting good peripheral view. Lenses should be distortion-free and made of a shatterproof material (the latter is essential for mountain bikers.) A neutral grey, green or blue tint is best for bright daylight, while clear or amber lenses are recommended for cloudy or rainy weather.

Cycle jerseys

Cycle jerseys have several advantages over T-shirts. They're made of fabrics that wick moisture away from the body to speed evaporation, preventing you from feeling cold and clammy in cool weather, while during warm weather jerseys keep you from overheating.

Training aids

Many cycle magazines advertise gadgets which the manufacturers claim will make you a better rider. In reality, there are really only two proven aids to the cyclist in serious training: the heart rate monitor and the cycle computer. Knowing how hard, how far, how fast and how long your cycling has been can be a great help in adding interest to your rides and maintaining your motivation.

Cycle computers

Cycle computers are mostly small, flat multi-functional instruments which attach to the handlebar (or, when integrated with a heart monitor, are worn on the wrist) and provide feedback on your performance in a variety of ways. They work via magnets attached to the wheel spokes and a sensor attached to the fork blade or chainstay. The computer is set for the diameter of the wheel. Each time it senses the magnet passing, it performs the necessary calculations for a readout on the display.

Heart rate monitors

The heart rate monitor uses a chest strap with an inbuilt sensor to detect the electrical activity of the heart muscle. It then transmits this information to the wristwatch receiver, where it appears in beats per minute. The rate at which your heart beats is a good indicator of the amount of oxygen that your whole body is processing. While there is no machine to tell you what your oxygen consumption is while cycling, you can use a heart rate monitor to give you a good indication and adjust your programme accordingly. The basic models are of use to any fitness enthusiast; the more expensive memory models are really only appropriate for dedicated racing cyclists.

A new breed of heart rate monitor has become available which combines the functions of a heart rate monitor and a cycle computer. Obviously, an ability to download such a variety of data from training rides and races enables you to monitor and analyse your performance in detail. These can be great for dedicated cyclists wanting an in-depth analysis of how they are training.

4 Riding techniques and safety

With any training programme, it is important to have a good grasp of the necessary safety precautions and technical considerations that will make it as risk-free and effective as possible. This chapter examines the key issues of basic riding technique, on- and off-road safety, and bicycle maintenance. Depending on your chosen activity, it may not all apply to you; but for the sake of your and other people's welfare, it is a good idea to make sure you are aware of the content.

Basic riding techniques

General

Starting and stopping

Most people discover that they favour one particular leg to start pedalling. If you use toe-clips or cleats, wait until you are safely through a junction or onto a road before you clip in with both feet.

When stopping, make your intentions clear to other road users. Apply your brakes and as you slow to a standstill, remove your left foot from the pedal and place it on the pavement. Alternatively, slide forward off the saddle and lower an unclipped foot to the ground.

Correct pedalling

You should aim to pedal at a constant speed – ideally, between 70 and 90 pedal revolutions per minute. The novice may need to build

> **Cycling is an easy way to keep fit, without the disadvantage of having to pay gym membership fees. I find that I am too busy looking at the scenery to notice that I am doing any work!**
>
> *Claire, a cyclist for 2 years*

up to this gradually. Persevere, and you will be a much smoother, more efficient cyclist as a result. As the route steepens or descends, use changes of gear to maintain this pedal speed – a lower gear on hills, a higher gear on descents.

So, at 8 mph or 28 mph your pedalling speed should be the same, with your choice of gear determining the speed at which you're travelling. In this way your cycling will be most effective and you will experience optimal fitness gains.

Relax and keep comfortable

Efficiency on the bike is influenced by how relaxed and comfortable you are while riding. Assuming that you're riding a properly sized and adjusted bike, maintain your comfort by changing hand position often, keeping your elbows relaxed, and gently stretching out your neck and shoulder throughout your session.

Cycling in the city

Knowing how to handle the various traffic situations in reasonable safety and with efficiency is essential; learning basic traffic skills removes one impediment to cycling as a fitness, recreational and sports activity.

Positioning on the road

Traffic laws in the UK direct cyclists to ride 'as far to the left as is possible'. (Reverse this and the following advice for countries where you drive on the right.) You should ride far enough to the left to allow traffic to pass, if it's safe for you to do so. And it is up to you to decide whether or not it's safe.

Desired positioning when cycling on the road

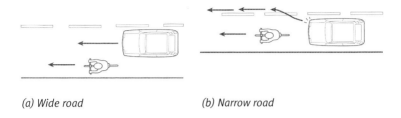

(a) Wide road   *(b) Narrow road*

Because bicycles are narrow, it is often possible to share a traffic lane with another vehicle (see above, (a)). However, if the lane is too narrow for you to share safely, ride far enough to the right to fully occupy the lane. Where the left-side wheel of cars would be is a good spot (see above, (b)), most often free from debris which could cause a puncture. Overtaking motorists will not be able to squeeze past you while remaining in the lane. Overtaking cyclists could still share the lane, so don't assume that you own the lane while riding in this blocking position. Always look behind you before moving left or right within the lane.

In a very wide lane there might be room for you to ride several feet from the curb and still allow room for traffic to pass to your right. Don't move left in this situation – you're safer away from the curb; you're more visible; there is more time to react to someone opening a car door or pulling out of a driveway; you're not holding up traffic; and there is less rubbish on the road which could cause a puncture. If there are parked cars or other barriers that form a 'wall' near the left edge of the road, move to the right. Give yourself room to manoeuvre and time to react to conditions like a sudden gust of wind or the impatient motorist who tries to squeeze past you in the lane.

If you are moving as fast as other traffic, move right into the lane. You won't hold anyone up and you need extra space around you at higher speeds. If you are grinding up a hill at little more than walking pace, move left. At slow speeds it is possible to ride safely within a few inches of the edge of the pavement, though you should always be watchful for glass and other debris.

At road junctions your position in the lane can be a very effective indication for other drivers as to which way you are going. If you are going straight or turning right, move to the centre or right-hand side of the lane. Drivers behind you who want to turn left can then pull up on your left and make the turn without crossing your path (see opposite, a). If you are turning left, keep left, await your turn and when it is safe to do so (see opposite, b).

Finally, always follow the rules of the road. Stop at stop signs. Be predictable. There is nothing more delightful than the look of astonishment on the face of a motorist when a cyclist correctly yields to them. Let's be our own best advertisement for our right to share the road.

On the open road

Coping with descents

When riding on- or off-road you must be in control of your speed. This requires continuous attention and concentration. Inevitably, you will be faced with a steep descent at some stage, and it is important that you are aware of safe riding. Always pay attention to the route rather than the scenery. There may be potholes, gravel, all kinds of hazards around the next corner. Maintain a comfortable speed to enable you to avoid these dangers.

Long descents may require frequent braking, so apply firm, uniform pressure to the front and rear brakes. Once you have reduced your speed, release them. Constant application of the brakes will overheat the rims and may cause a tyre to burst. If your bike begins to wobble during a fast descent, stay calm. The geometry of some bike frames and forks (wheels out of true or loose components) may cause your bike to shake at high speeds. If this occurs, continue to apply your brakes intermittently until you have slowed down – the wobble should subside at a lower speed. When you have come to a complete stop check your bike for mechanical problems.

Desired positioning at road junctions

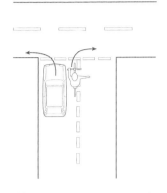

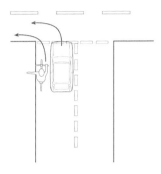

(c) Road junctions turning right   *(d) Road junctions turning left*

It is tempting to freewheel on descents, but continuing to pedal when riding downhill serves an important training function. It aids the removal of waste products from the muscles, and the return of de-oxygenated blood to the heart.

Descending around corners

As you approach a corner, slow down while you're still travelling upright in a straight line, so you don't have to brake as you're leaning over. Apply more braking force to the front brake as long as you are upright and travelling in a straight line. Braking during a curve may cause skidding and loss of control. Ride with your body in an upright position in the saddle. This will create additional air resistance and will help to slow your speed. Keep both hands on the handlebar.

Remember to remain in the same relative portion of the lane when riding a curvy descent. When a corner is so tight that it requires you to stop pedalling and freewheel, straighten your outside leg, pedal down, and apply some pressure on this outside pedal – this will enhance your grip and stability in the corner. Be very aware of the centrifugal forces on tight curves, which will send you away from the apex of the corner.

Riding in the rain

Wet roads require greater attention to the above techniques: you must control your speed even more. Roads are slippery when wet, and your brakes are much less effective. At times you may need to keep a constant, light pressure on the brakes to sweep the water off the rims so you'll have some braking power. If you get caught in the rain, always use extreme caution.

Off-roading

If you have chosen to use a mountain bike to gain or improve personal fitness and you intend to venture off-road onto rough, there will be obstacles along the way which must be overcome – indeed, it is these very obstacles which make riding off-road as challenging and enjoyable as it is! Most importantly, look where you want to go. Your bike follows your head. Scan the track ahead, letting your eyes rove from 15 m, to 10 m, to 5 m and then to 2 m in front of you before looking ahead again. Know what's coming and pick your line accordingly. Don't look at the things you don't want to crash into, because you will find yourself deviating towards them.

Riding over obstacles

If you're out on the trail, sooner or later you're going to have to ride over something. The great thing about a mountain bike is that it's designed to get over obstacles easily. You, as pilot, just need to remember some helpful pointers.

- You will often need speed to get over things, otherwise an obstacle will stop you dead when you hit it and you risk falling. Remember to keep your speed up until you're only a couple of feet away from the obstacle. If heading uphill, you're going to need to keep pedalling until you clear the obstacle, and then keep pedalling afterwards.

- Many mountain bikes are fitted with front and sometimes rear suspension, but your body is the biggest and best shock-absorber. Use it to your advantage. Loosen up.

■ As you approach the obstacle, transfer your weight through your legs onto your pedals. Keep your hands off the brakes. Use the handlebars to steer you directly perpendicular to the obstacle. Move your bottom slightly up off the seat. Move back slightly.

Absorbing the obstacle

■ When you reach the obstacle, shift your weight to the rear of the bike and keep a solid grip on the handlebars. Keep the front wheel straight at all costs. When the front wheel hits, absorb the impact by bending your elbows and knees. The front wheel will rise towards your body: let it come (see opposite, top).

Moving your weight forwards

■ After your front wheel makes it over, straighten your arms by pushing the handlebars away from you. Don't lock your elbows, just move them to a straighter angle. This helps move your weight forwards on to the front tyre again (see opposite, middle). Now stay off the saddle and let the rear wheel roll over the obstacle (see opposite, bottom). The bike's over, you're over. Scan the trail ahead, put your rear back on the seat, stay loose, and enjoy the ride.

Rear wheel over

Dealing with dogs

Dogs love cyclists – they love chasing them! Providing advice on how to deal with dogs in every situation is impossible. Different dogs have different personalities, and opinion differs on how to cope with them. Many dogs will retreat if you just shout 'No!' or 'Home!' Other 'scare' tactics include pretending to throw something or spraying the dog in the face from your water bottle. Some people suggest talking to the dog in a quiet, calm voice. More drastic measures like kicking are not recommended because you will lose control of your bike.

Whatever method you choose when dealing with a dog, avoid hitting it with your front wheel. If your wheel is diverted, you are likely to fall; and while most people worry more about being bitten, dogs tend to cause injuries to cyclists much more frequently by causing falls. If and when you come upon that 'mad dog', keep both feet on the pedals, both hands on the handlebars, and be ready to apply the brakes. Only after your front wheel is past the dog should you worry about being bitten.

Climbing hills

Don't ride up hills, ride over hills. Inexperienced cyclists faced with hills tend to shift into lower gears as they progress higher, gradually slowing down and fading completely at the top. Most experienced riders shift into bigger gears as they go, gradually speeding up near the top, and maintaining this speed after the hill stops. The key is to pace yourself from the bottom of the hill. Never avoid hills when riding. They are the key to both aerobic conditioning (see p. 52) and developing muscle strength and endurance.

Climbing hills requires a little preparation, but the key is to get comfortable. Your position, the gear you select and the speed at which you travel will affect your ability to reach the top in one piece. You need to look ahead, take stock of the hill, and try to judge a few key things.

- What front chain-ring should you be in, given your strength and the steepness of the hill? If it's really steep and long, shift down into the smallest chain-ring. If it's medium, maybe the middle one. Your left hand controls this.

Correct position for climbing steep hills

- It's important to shift into the chain-ring you want to climb in before you start uphill, otherwise you can run into problems. If you need to, work your way down the smaller gears as you climb.

- As you shift, make sure you're pedalling smoothly. Do not stop pedalling, shift the gear, then start pedalling again – you should aim to shift without putting climbing pressure on the chain. Also, try not to change the big chain-ring as you climb. If you do need to go down to a lower gear, make sure it's a smooth transition, without pressure on the chain.

Overall, you want to be pedalling smoothly and efficiently. It should be hard work, but not impossible. Stay seated if you can. And initially, don't be ashamed to get off and walk if the going gets too tough!

Steep descents

The exhilaration you can gain from riding a mountain bike down-hill at speed is the reward for the effort required to reach the top of the hill! On normal descents the same rules apply as for road descents (see pp. 30–1). However, when things get really steep you need some different techniques.

- Move your body weight further back. In some cases, you may need to slide all the way off the back of the saddle – practise this skill.

- Stop pedalling. Keep your pedals horizontal to avoid catching

your lower foot on any-
thing, and ensure that your
weight is on the balls of
your feet and stabilised
through your thigh mus-
cles. Do not lock your
knees – your legs are the
ultimate shock-absorber.
Extend your arms (almost
fully) in a relaxed position.
Do not lock them.

Correct position for steep descents

- Try to steer by shifting your
hips and bodyweight rather
than the wheel. If you do use the wheel, turn it very slowly and
smoothly.

- To brake, use the rear and 'pump' the front. Be careful not to lock
the brakes, especially the front.

- Finally, start slowly. There is no need to go fast until you really
start to master the required skills.

Bicycle maintenance

When you go for a bike ride your body will get a workout, and so
will your bike. Have you checked your bike for mechanical safety?
Timely bicycle maintenance can prevent a serious accident. Here is
a series of checks which you should carry out every time you ride.

Your wheels

Check the tyre pressure. Tyres should be inflated to the rated pressure noted on the sidewall (pounds per square inch, or bar). Use
a gauge to verify that you have reached the recommended rate –
if you don't have a floor pump with a gauge, use the finger tests,
as follows:

- A road bike tyre should be inflated until it won't deform when
you try to press your thumb into the tread.

The off-road code

There are several well-established rules that all mountain bikers should learn:

- Ride on legally open trails only. You must not ride on public footpaths
- Don't leave evidence of your passing, for example, on certain soils after a rain storm. Practise low-impact cycling. Stay on existing tracks and do not create new ones
- Ride in control. Control is the key to fun riding
- Yield the trail to other users, including walkers and horses. Make your approach well known. A friendly greeting or bell is considerate and works well; don't startle others. Anticipate other trail-users around corners or in blind spots
- Never scare animals. Give animals extra room and time to adjust to you. When passing horses, use special care and follow directions from the riders (ask if uncertain). Worrying cattle and disturbing wildlife are serious offences
- Leave gates as you find them – or as marked
- Plan ahead. Make sure you have all the equipment you need. Be self-sufficient at all times, keep your equipment in good repair, and carry necessary supplies for changes in weather or other conditions. Always wear a helmet when riding off-road, and ride with a friend

- A mountain bike tyre should deform by 3–4 mm when you try to press your thumb into the tread.

Check for damage to the tyre sidewalls and the tread. Sidewall damage is common if the brakes aren't adjusted properly. If the bands of the tyre are showing below the surface, you need a new tyre.

Your quick releases

These are the means of attaching the wheels to the frame. Quick-release hubs need to be tight, but not too tight. The proper pressure is obtained by pushing on the quick-release lever so it leaves an impression on the palm of your hand. The closed lever should face up and back to minimise the chance of catching on anything while you ride. Quick-release brakes, which are opened when removing or installing wheels, need to be in the closed position. When closed, check to make sure the brake pads aren't rubbing the rims.

Your brakes

Look at the brake-block pad for wear. If less than 2 mm of rubber shows at any place, replace the brake-block or pad assembly. Make sure the brake blocks are almost parallel and aligned with the side of the rim when applied (the front area of the pad should contact the rim first by 1 mm). Check the cables and housing. Cables need to travel smoothly. If they stick, apply lubrication at the ends of the housing and work it in by applying the brakes several times. Replace frayed cables.

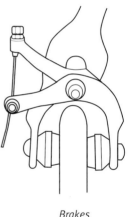

Brakes

Your drivetrain

Check the crank set. This consists of the bottom bracket, the crank arms, and the chain-rings. To do this, take the left and right crank arms in your hands and attempt to move them sideways. If both move, you have a problem with the bottom bracket. If only one moves, the individual crank arm is loose and must be secured. A loose crank arm should never be ridden.

Finish your pre-ride checks with a brief, slow ride to check that your gear derailleurs and shift levers are working properly. If you find that your bike needs adjustments beyond your ability, enlist the mechanics at your local bike shop – don't risk riding it until faults have been successfully remedied.

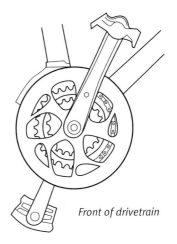

Front of drivetrain

5 Planning your training programme

Training principles

Before looking specifically at cycling for fitness, it is important to consider the basic principles behind the start of any exercise programme. To build fitness training into your lifestyle, and to benefit fully from its effects, you have got to make a commitment – to have real 'staying-power'. However, it is also important to decide quite early on what level of fitness you want to achieve. Fitness is a very personal matter. Though you may be restricted by such factors as age and genetics, you can greatly improve the quality of your life by initiating and maintaining a balanced exercise routine, and at the same time improving your nutrition.

Before going any further down your chosen route to fitness, you should first establish that your basic health is able to withstand an increase in your level of physical activity.

Checking your health

It is generally accepted that vigorous exercise involves minimal health risks for people in good health or those under medical supervision. Far greater risks are presented by habitual inactivity and obesity. As a rule, if you are under 35 and in good health, you probably do not need to see a doctor before beginning an exercise programme. However, if you are over 35 – and especially if you have been inactive for several years – you should consult your physician, who may or may not recommend a graded exercise test. There are certain conditions in particular that indicate a need for medical supervision or clearance.

Conditions requiring medical clearance

- high blood pressure
- heart trouble
- dizzy spells
- breathlessness after mild exertion
- arthritis or other bone and joint disorders

If you know that you suffer from any of these conditions or you are pregnant, you are already likely to be under medical supervision. Otherwise, you can gain some indication by carrying out a quick self-check. Start by answering the questions below.

- Has your doctor ever said that you have a heart condition and that you should only do physical activity as recommended by a doctor?
- Do you feel pain in your chest when you do physical activity?
- In the past month, have you had chest pain when you were not doing physical activity?
- Do you lose your balance because of dizziness or do you ever lose consciousness?
- Do you have a bone or joint problem that could be made worse by a change in your physical activity?
- Is your doctor currently prescribing drugs for your blood pressure or heart condition?
- Do you know of any other reason why you should not do physical activity?
- Are you pregnant?
- Do you suffer from diabetes?
- Do you suffer from epilepsy?

If you answered 'Yes' to one or more of the above questions, it is very important that you talk to your doctor before you start a training programme – or increase the intensity of an existing one. Remember, the above is only designed to give you an indication; if in any doubt, consult your doctor.

> I like cycling because it has made me stronger – physically, mentally and emotionally. A long, solo training ride makes you realise your body is a lot tougher than you thought it was and riding in a pack encourages you to trust others.
>
> *Chris, a cyclist for 20 years*

Goal-setting and motivation

To plan an effective training programme you must first establish what you want to achieve, and to set yourself targets or goals to aim for. At its simplest, the process of goal-setting allows you to choose what you want to achieve at the end of a period of training. By knowing this, you know what to concentrate on and improve. Goal-setting gives you long-term vision and short-term motivation. If you set sharp, clearly-defined goals, you will see progress in what might otherwise have seemed a long and pointless grind. By setting goals effectively you can almost certainly improve performance by improving the quality of your training, increasing your motivation to achieve greater results and improving your self-confidence in coping with challenging training situations.

The first step is to decide your level of commitment to your activity, then write down a list of your more specific targets. You may find the following guidelines useful.

After achieving your goals?

Enjoy the satisfaction of having done it. If the goal was a significant one, or one that you had worked towards for some time, then reward yourself.

Guidelines for setting training goals

- Set positive goals, rather than an attempt 'not to do something'.
- Be precise. If you set a precise goal, put in dates, times and other details so that achievement can be measured.
- Set out your goals in order of priority, otherwise you can become overwhelmed.
- Set your goals at the right level. Set them so that they are slightly out of range of your current ability, but not so high that there is no hope of achieving them; no one will put serious effort into achieving a goal that they believe is unrealistic.
- Set goals over which you have as much control as possible. There is nothing more depressing than failing to achieve a personal goal for reasons beyond your control such as poor judging, bad weather, injury, etc.
- Set specific, measurable goals. If you achieve all the conditions of a measurable goal, then you can be confident and comfortable in its achievement.

Having achieved a goal, it should influence your next ones. If the goal was easily achieved, make your next goals harder. If the goal took a depressingly long time to achieve, make the next target a little easier. If you learned something that indicates the need to revise the targets you still have outstanding, then do so. If while achieving the goal you still noticed some deficit in your armoury, set goals to fix this. Remember too that goals change as you change. Adjust them regularly to reflect changes in your fitness, skill, or even level of enthusiasm. If goals do not hold any attraction any longer then let them go – goal-setting for performance should be your servant, not your master.

Motivation

It is sometimes hard to maintain your motivation to train, but it can help to make training a habit. Doing things regularly can make difficult tasks easy, but don't become a slave to your schedule. Try the tips on pages 46–7 to keep your training enjoyable.

Planning your training

The warm-up and cool-down

When planning any training programme, you must build in as a matter of course two key components: a thorough, effective warm-up before, and cool-down after, every session. These are a vital part of both preparation and ongoing performance. The general principles are discussed here, with stretching and massage being covered in depth in the following chapter.

An ideal warm-up would consist of 10–12 minutes of easy to moderate riding, followed by stretching the muscles in the lower back, legs, neck and shoulder – see Chapter 6, pp. 82–8. A further 5 minutes of riding – with the heart rate being gradually raised to the target levels of the training session – would finish off the warm-up. A warm-up is important even in hot weather – increasing the core temperature of muscles requires activity. Ensure that you have developed a light sweat and slightly laboured breathing before training harder in the heat.

If you are going to undertake an intensive interval training session, you should aim in your warm-up to raise your intensity and heart rate gradually to levels close to those anticipated in the main workout. This can be achieved after a continuous, sustained ride of between 10 and 15 minutes at around 65 per cent maximum. After this period, introduce some 10-second maximal efforts, with 50 seconds recovery between each one. After five to six sprints, you should be ready to start the main interval session, well warmed-up and ready for action.

> There is nothing better than working hard to cycle up a hill, only to feel the wind rushing past you as you go down the other side.
>
> *Robert, a cyclist for 20 years*

Guidelines for motivation

- Look at your schedule realistically. How many days are you willing to commit to an exercise programme? How long per workout? Incorporate those workout times into your schedule. Don't be discouraged or disappointed if you miss a day. More is not necessarily better. The keys to developing a lifetime habit of regular exercise are slow progression, consistency, and regularity. Identify any other obstacles that may prevent you from exercising and find ways to work around them. Try to set aside specific times to ride, and keep to them, no matter what. This will give you a sense of responsibility, and give your fitness the priority it deserves.

- Select an activity that you enjoy, one that you feel you will want to participate in regularly. Find something you truly enjoy doing, and there's a greater likelihood you'll stick to it.

- Keep a training diary, recording the activity performed, date, time of day, duration of activity, and how you felt upon completion. This reinforces your cycling as a habit, rather than a task. If you think of exercise as non-negotiable, like going to work or school, you will just do it, and you're more likely to stay motivated.

- Choose something that's both achievable and gives you a sense of triumph in the end, but don't be too ambitious. Set 'mini-goals' on the road towards your ultimate goal, and give yourself the credit you deserve when you reach them.

- Exercise with a friend: you'll motivate each other and maintain regularity in exercise participation. To achieve long-term success, you need support. You'll be more likely to stick with your programme if someone is offering encouragement and sharing your pitfalls and triumphs.

- Reward yourself after participating in an activity for a certain number of days.

- Include sufficient rest days in your training. This will help to avoid injuries and prevent the symptoms of overtraining. Scheduling rest days will not take anything away from your progress. Rather, rest days allow your body to function and make more efficient and rapid progress. Pain is a signal to the body that something is wrong. If you feel pain or become over-exhausted while training, consult your coach or your physician as appropriate.
- Finally, don't be afraid to seek advice. You can never know it all, and the 'expert' whom you approach won't know it all either!

The cool-down is the recovery phase – the point at which you start to recover from the workout you have just finished. It is almost guaranteed that if you do not cool down and stretch after a strenuous workout, you could be in a lot of pain for the next day or two.

Once you have lowered your heart rate through gentle riding, you should aim to stretch all your muscles – paying special attention to the muscles you've just worked. Each cool-down stretch should last between 8 and 15 seconds and you should hold the stretch a little longer and repeat it if the muscle feels particularly stiff or sore. Don't overdo the stretching; simply stretch until you feel some mild tension in the muscle. Remember: stretching shouldn't hurt. We will examine cycling specific stretches in more detail in Chapter 6.

Creating a training schedule

Creating a training schedule is an excellent way to organise your cycling. With a well-thought-out schedule, you'll have a better sense of where you're headed and how you're going to get there. A good programme should also motivate you. Following your day-to-day progress is enjoyable and encouraging. In time, your schedule will become more than an organisational tool – it becomes a challenge and a reward in itself.

The trick is to put together the right schedule. If you set your sights too high, you'll soon get frustrated. If you aim too low, you won't be motivated. Don't get locked into the specific elements of your schedule – let them evolve. If you have a ride scheduled one weekend but something comes up, don't worry about it. You want a schedule that's specific enough to keep you interested, but not so specific that you get bogged down in the details. Finally, maintaining a schedule shouldn't be so involved and time-consuming that you quickly tire of it. When in doubt, simplify and stick to the basics. The steps listed below will help you to create the right plan for you.

Identify your base fitness level

The guidelines given on pp. 49–50 will enable you to establish your base fitness level, and to pitch your training schedule appropriately (see also pp. 54–9, 'Sample training programmes').

Identify your training opportunities

Consider how much time you have to train each week (see also Planning your programme, below). Be honest, and don't forget to include the time it takes to get ready for a ride, to change and shower afterwards. Bear in mind your work and family commitments, and factors such as availability of equipment. Schedule your workouts for a time when there is little chance that you will have to cancel or interrupt them because of other demands on your time.

Identify any obstacles

What would make it hard for you to maintain a training programme? Lack of equipment, lack of time, lack of support, adverse weather? Although you should be aware of these, there are always ways around any obstacle; it won't always be easy, but if you have truly made a commitment, you will find a way. (See also pp. 60–3 below on 'Problem-solving'.)

Plan your programme – general considerations

If you can find time for 3 x 30 minute sessions each week, you can improve your fitness through cycling. More than that is a bonus –

30 minutes each day would be excellent, and an hour each day fantastic. But start slowly: if you are new to training, 3 x 30 minutes is a good starting point.

As a general rule, train by gradually increasing the duration of rides, then the intensity, then combine the two, then recover. This works out nicely as a three-week build-up period, followed by a one-week recovery period. The following gives a sample four-week progression at a basic level.

Sample 4-week training progression

Week	Progression
Week 1	Ride further than you normally do
Week 2	Ride over your normal distance, but at a higher intensity
Week 3	Ride the distances you covered in Week 1, at the intensity of Week 2
Week 4	Ride half the distance of Week 3, at the intensity of Week 2

How often, how long and how hard you exercise within a schedule should be determined both by your goals and by your present fitness level. Look at the following four broad fitness levels, and decide which most closely fits your own. Then, follow the relevant general guidelines to help you build up your weekly schedule. (Note: the ride durations given do not include the warm-up or cool-down.)

Fitness level 1
You never (or rarely) participate in aerobic activity.

At this level, most experts recommend beginning with three sessions per week, 20–30 minutes per session. If you cannot ride for 20 minutes to begin with, don't worry, just keep at it until you do reach the 20-minute mark. The key is to begin slowly and gradually work up to more exercise. People who jump from doing nothing right into exercising five or six times a week will burn out and probably injure themselves. If you are using an exercise bike indoors, boredom and discomfort will be the main enemies. The first time you train, see how long you can go before you get fed up with it. Then for your actual programme, just aim to do 80 per cent of this time. This way, you know that you won't get bored each time you start a fitness session.

Fitness level 2

You comfortably participate in aerobic activity for at least 20 minutes three times per week.

Try to increase the duration of your rides to 30 minutes and try to exercise four times a week (rather than three). If you've been doing 20 minutes of exercise, try increasing the duration in small increments (i.e. 22 minutes, then 24 minutes, etc.), rather than increasing the duration by the full 10 minutes – this will make the transition easier.

Fitness level 3

You can ride comfortably for at least 30 minutes, 3–4 times per week.

To increase your level of fitness, try to exercise for 30 minutes 4–5 times per week, if four times, increase to five. Build progression into your plan. You could ride the same distance as usual but try to do it faster, or ride further in the same time. Any of these methods will help to maintain a positive physical stress on your body.

Fitness level 4

You are a regular recreational cyclist who can ride comfortably for more than one hour, more than four times per week.

At this level, your most appropriate means of increasing fitness is to undertake a programme that is based on training for competition. The competitive approach will introduce new training stresses, which will elicit greater gains than could be achieved by simply continuing your recreational-style fitness training, even if you don't want to compete.

Every workout should begin with a warm-up and end with a cool-down (see pp. 45–7). Never be tempted to skip them! Finally, as a general rule, space your workouts throughout the week and avoid consecutive days of hard exercise.

Types of training session

To understand the principles behind the sample training programmes given in the following pages, we should look in a little more detail at the three essential ingredients of fast recreational riding: base endurance, aerobic conditioning and aerobic power. Improvements in these components will bring hours of enjoyment while cycling, and potential progression to higher training levels as discussed in Chapter 8.

Training to improve base endurance

Endurance, simply put, is the ability to persist in exercise – to resist fatigue. Building a solid 'base' of endurance fitness comes from time in the saddle and is best gained through long, steady rides away from major climbs.

Base endurance takes a while to develop – around 100 hours of riding for the complete newcomer to cycling. However, just like the foundations of a building, it provides an essential framework to support efficient and effective heart, lungs and muscles. In building base endurance, you are in effect getting fit before you start to train.

Keep your endurance rides low in intensity and do them for as long as you can manage. If you're starting from scratch, 20–30 minutes, three times a week is plenty to begin with (see pp. 49–50). Such rides have two major benefits:

■ They increase fitness without the pain and discomfort that accompanies high intensity riding
■ They teach muscles to burn fat.

On endurance rides, the pace should be kept steady and the effort feel comfortable, with a heart rate of below 60–65 per cent max. By taking the time to build such a base, you will progress much faster when the time comes to increase riding intensity – you'll reach your potential a lot quicker.

Training to improve aerobic conditioning

After the 'skeleton' of base fitness comes the 'meat' of aerobic conditioning (sometimes known as aerobic development). The intensity of rides can be increased now, the primary aim being a general improvement in heart and muscle efficiency.

To gain aerobic condition you'll need to start to work or 'stress' the heart. This means bringing the riding intensity up from base fitness levels of around 60–65 per cent max, to closer to 75–80 per cent max – equivalent to a moderate-to-high training load, as shown in the sample training patterns on pp. 55–9. The best means of raising your heart rate on a bike is simply to head for the hills (see pp. 34–6). Otherwise, ride hard periodically over mixed terrain. Just enjoy the feeling! Anything that will raise your heart rate – preferably for at least 10 minutes – before you settle the pace down again will have substantial benefits.

When you have accumulated around 40 hours of riding to improve aerobic conditioning, you will be ready to introduce sessions specifically designed to develop aerobic power.

Training to improve aerobic power (VO2max)

Also known as aerobic capacity or 'VO2max', this element of fitness may be defined as maximum oxygen uptake. Aerobic power training sessions are designed to improve the heart's ability to deliver oxygen to active muscle. Such sessions can help develop speed when done on the flat, or climbing power when the efforts are made over hilly terrain.

Interval training (where you 'sandwich' periods of intense physical activity between periods of recovery, which allows longer periods of training at high intensity) is one of the most efficient ways in which to develop aerobic power. This is because when your heart beats, a certain volume of blood (which is carrying oxygen to the muscle) is pumped from the left lower chamber of the heart – the left ventricle. The amount of blood pumped per heartbeat is called stroke volume. The greatest stimulus for placing stress on your stroke volume – and thus enabling adaptation – occurs immediately after a short, very high-intensity period of exercise. Therefore, intensive bursts of riding will encourage greater adaptation; and building in a recovery period between these efforts will allow you to do a greater number of intensive bursts.

Interval training is also a very powerful means of reducing body fat by devouring calories, suppressing appetite and raising heat production and fat burning levels post-exercise.

As a result of improving base endurance and aerobic conditioning, you should now be able to ride very hard for 30 seconds. For your aerobic power session, warm up for 15 minutes by doing a ride at about 65 per cent max. Then do your 30-second hard effort – and it should feel hard. Then ride easily for 30 seconds, then hard again, and so on. After five efforts – known as 'repetitions' – you can have a much longer rest, say 5 minutes of gentle riding. Try to do a further two sets of 5 x 30 seconds, with a 30-second recovery between efforts and five minutes between sets. An interval session such as this will create the stimulus for beneficial adaptations in the heart no fewer than 15 times in just 25 minutes of riding!

Two such sessions each week – and that should be the maximum that you attempt – will enable you to ride further and faster than ever before.

Specific planning

Sample training patterns

When planning your schedule, you should decide how to divide the overall training load. The tables on pp. 55–9 give some sample training 'patterns', each of which is linked to the four different fitness levels identified on pp. 49–50. Once you have established which level most closely relates to you, refer to the relevant training pattern.

These sample training patterns are intended only as a general guide. Don't consider them as strict rules to be followed implicitly – you'll need to change your routine over time to allow both sufficient overload, and the necessary recuperation, for a progressive increase in fitness. For example, a rider at level four may well use the first pattern as a recovery week; the rider at level two may attempt level four as a challenge.

Sample training programmes

Optimal training requires a balance of work, or 'stress', and rest. Likewise, the body needs to stay in balance throughout each weekly or monthly cycle of training. As a result, it is important to employ a weekly training schedule that keeps your body well rested while ensuring that progress is made.

Obviously, your own commitments in respect of work, social life, recreation and family will strongly shape your programme. Therefore, just as with the training patterns given in the tables, the following training programmes are intended as an aid to planning. They should be used in conjunction with your personal circumstances – thus enabling you to work out a training programme to suit you.

Sample training programme for fitness level 1 (p. 55)

The training progresses from three 20-minute rides each week, to the addition of hilly routes, longer rides, and longer hilly rides, with the 8-week period leading to an increase in riding time from 60 to 140 minutes per week. You will see that there is no recovery week. At this point in a rider's development, the adaptations to training can occur rapidly and after an initial period of adjustment, full recovery often occurs after a full day's rest. The addition of an extra ride in week four places additional demands on the rider; but as the subsequent sessions are after a day of rest, and are either short hilly or easy rides, there should be no problem adapting.

Sample 8-week programme – fitness level 1

	Mon	Tue	Wed	Thur	Fri	Sat	Sun
Week 1		Easy 20 min ride. Flat		Easy 20 min ride. Flat			Easy 20 min ride. Flat
Week 2		Easy 20 min ride. Flat		Easy 30 min ride. Flat			Easy 20 min ride. Flat
Week 3		Easy 30 min ride. Flat		Easy 20 min ride. Flat			Easy 30 min ride. Flat
Week 4		Easy 30 min ride. Flat		Easy 20 min ride. Flat		Easy 20 min ride. Flat	Easy 30 min ride. Flat
Week 5		Easy 20 min ride. Hilly		Easy 30 min ride. Flat		Easy 20 min ride. Hilly	Easy 30 min ride. Flat
Week 6		Easy 30 min ride. Flat		Easy 20 min ride. Flat		Easy 20 min ride. Hilly	Easy 45 min ride. Flat
Week 7		Easy 45 min ride. Flat		Easy 20 min ride. Hilly		Easy 30 min ride. Flat	Easy 45 min ride. Flat
Week 8		Easy 30 min ride. Flat		Easy 40 min ride. Hilly		Easy 30 min ride. Flat	Easy 40 min ride. Hilly

Sample training programme for fitness level 2 (p. 57)

The training progresses from 20-minute rides each week, to the addition of hilly routes, longer rides, and longer hilly rides, with the 8-week period leading to an increase in riding time to three hours per week. The training progression is not always reliant on riding harder and harder. You will see that week 8 contains no hilly or hard rides, the training load coming from the duration of the rides, totalling three hours.

Sample training programme for fitness level 3 (p. 58)

This plan leads the rider through two distinct phases of training: weeks 1–3 and weeks 5–7. Weeks 4 and 8 are recovery weeks. The first period develops fitness through intensity with combinations of hard rides. The second period uses an increase in the duration of easy rides as the main source of training progression.

Sample training programme for fitness level 4 (p. 59)

For more experienced cyclists, this plan allows just one day off each week, though Monday is set aside as an easy day. Again, weeks 4 and 8 are set aside for recovery, though they still require at least 150 minutes per week on the bike. As fitness progresses, a rider can still recover from hard training even when required to do sustained endurance rides.

Keep a training diary

Keep a record of your training – what you have done, as well as what your longer-term intentions are. A daily training log should record anything which is likely to affect your performance – your diet, the quality of the previous night's sleep, weather conditions, etc. In this way, exceptional rides (bad or good) can be better explained by referring to these various factors in your diary. The example on p. 60 uses check-boxes to record relevant data quickly and easily, and although it is merely a suggestion, it could be photocopied and used.

Sample 8-week programme – fitness level 2

	Mon	Tue	Wed	Thur	Fri	Sat	Sun
Week 1		Hilly 30 min ride.		Easy 20 min ride. Flat	Hilly 30 min ride		Easy 45 min ride. Flat
Week 2		Hilly 30 min ride.	Easy 20 min ride. Flat	Hilly 30 min ride.			Easy 45 min ride. Flat
Week 3		Easy 45 min ride. Flat	Easy 20 min ride. Flat	Easy 45 min ride. Flat			Easy 45 min ride. Flat
Week 4		Hilly 30 min ride. Flat	Easy 30 min ride. Flat	Hilly 30 min ride. Flat			Easy 60 min ride. Flat
Week 5		Hilly 30 min ride.	Easy 30 min ride. Flat	Hilly 30 min ride. Flat			Easy 60 min ride. Flat
Week 6		Easy 45 min ride. Flat		Easy 45 min ride. Flat			Easy 60 min ride. Flat
Week 7		Easy 45 min ride. Flat	Easy 30 min ride. Flat	Easy 45 min ride. Flat		Hilly 30 min ride.	Easy 45 min ride. Flat
Week 8		Easy 30 min ride. Flat	Easy 60 min ride. Flat	Easy 30 min ride. Flat			Easy 60 min ride. Hilly

Sample 8-week programme – fitness level 3

	Mon	Tue	Wed	Thur	Fri	Sat	Sun
Week 1		Easy 45 min ride. Flat	Very hard, hilly 30 min ride.	Easy 45 min ride. Flat			Easy 60 min ride. Flat
Week 2		Easy 45 min ride. Flat	Very hard, hilly 30 min ride.	Easy 45 min ride. Flat			Easy 60 min ride. Flat
Week 3		Easy 45 min ride. Flat	Very hard, hilly 30 min ride.	Easy 45 min ride. Flat		Very hard, hilly 30 min ride.	Easy 60 min ride. Flat
Week 4		Easy 45 min ride. Flat		Easy 45 min ride. Flat			Easy 45 min ride. Flat
Week 5		Easy 60 min ride. Flat	Hilly 45 min ride.	Easy 45 min ride. Flat			Easy 70 min ride. Flat
Week 6		Easy 60 min ride. Flat	Hilly 45 min ride.	Easy 45 min ride. Flat	Very hard, hilly 30 min ride.		Easy 80 min ride. Flat
Week 7		Easy 60 min ride on flat route	Hilly 30 min ride.	Easy 45 min ride on flat route	Very hard, hilly 30 min ride.		Easy 80 min ride. Flat
Week 8		Easy 45 min ride. Flat		Easy 45 min ride. Flat			Easy 45 min ride. Hilly

Sample 8-week programme – fitness level 4

	Mon	Tue	Wed	Thur	Fri	Sat	Sun
Week 1	Easy 30 min ride. Flat	45 min hilly	60 min easy	Very hard, 30 min (or interval training)		45 min easy	60 min easy
Week 2	Easy 30 min ride. Flat	45 min hilly	60 min easy	Very hard, 30 min (or interval training)		45 min easy	60 min easy
Week 3	Easy 30 min ride. Flat	45 min hilly	60 min easy	Very hard, 45 min (or interval training)		45 min easy	60 min easy
Week 4	Easy 30 min ride. Flat	45 min easy	45 min hilly	45 min easy		45 min easy	45 min hilly
Week 5	Easy 30 min ride. Flat	Very hard, hilly 45 min	60 min easy	Very hard, hilly 45 min		60 min easy	Easy 70 min ride. Flat
Week 6	Easy 30 min ride. Flat	Very hard, hilly 45 min	80 min easy	Hard hilly 45 min		60 min easy	90 min easy
Week 7	Easy 30 min ride. Flat	Very hard, hilly 45 min	90 min easy	Hard hilly 45 min		60 min easy	100 min easy
Week 8		45 min easy		45 min easy			60 min easy

Example training diary

Cycling training diary	Date
Resting heart rate (BPM)	
Quality of sleep	
Quality of previous day's diet	
How do I 'feel?' (ranked 1–10)	
Training completed today	
How did I feel during training?	
Was my heart rate responding as I'd expect	
Route details	
Good/bad day's training?	
Race notes	

Problem-solving

It is more than likely that you will encounter some problems with your training at some point – often through no fault of your own. Perhaps you will find it difficult to fit your exercise in, or difficult to stay motivated. This section will help to identify and address such problems.

Time constraints

Fitting your training in around your commitments may be easier if you bear in mind the following advice.

- Explain your goals to your partner and discuss how they may affect your relationship and/or family, both positively and adversely.
- Be organised, so the rest of your life operates smoothly and all your other responsibilities are met.
- Try establishing a routine.
- Try letting something go. Are there low-priority activities you can

stop doing to make time for improving your fitness?

■ Pencil in training sessions on your daily calendar.

■ Consider lunch-break training. This may help you get the correct amount of training done each week.

The 'fitness plateau'

Many riders get to a certain fitness level then fail to see any further improvements. The root of the problem is that training, like many things in life, is affected by the 'law of diminishing returns'. This dictates that initially, upon starting to ride, you will see a slight dip in performance as your body adjusts to regular exercise. Then you will make quite rapid improvements in performance as the training starts to increase your body's efficiency. However, this period of rapid gain can be followed by a period where maximum efforts bring minute improvements or even decreased fitness levels.

The answer is to change – to do things a little differently. Individuals suffer this fitness plateau for different reasons. The most likely possibilities are as follows.

■ You may not be subjecting your body to sufficient training stress. When you started training, the distances and speeds which you rode each week were probably sufficient to stress your heart, lungs and muscles; therefore, your body adapted to the stress, and your fitness improved. However, if you fail to increase the training load progressively, no adaptation will occur and you will experience no further improvement. The answer is to step up the overall training volume slightly. Try and do your usual rides in less time, or take longer rides in the same time period by increasing your training intensity.

■ You may be training inconsistently. Perhaps you are training well for a few weeks, having a couple of months off, then training hard again. Just as your body adapts to training, it also adapts to de-training, so that in those couple of months off, you are undoing all your good work. Get consistency into your training, work on a four-week cycle: say, three weeks of consistent rides four times a week, and one week of inconsistent, 'train as you like' rides. That way you will be allowing your body time to recover.

■ Perhaps you're training too much, too frequently, too fast or too far, or a combination. By training too hard you won't be allowing your body to adapt to the stress of training and to recover sufficiently. If you are constantly tired, irritable, sleeping poorly, and are not seeing an improvement in your fitness, don't train harder – have a rest, then cut down the speed of your rides while maintaining the distances. You should see an improvement in a few weeks. If you are relatively new to cycling, you should also beware of increasing your mileage too quickly. Make sure you have developed a good base fitness, achieved by long slow rides, beforehand (see pp. 49–51).

■ Diet. Training uses energy which must be replaced through diet, and exercise places demands on systems in the body which are regulated by vitamins and minerals. As discussed in Chapter 7, your energy needs will be covered by a balanced diet consisting mainly of carbohydrates. Vitamin and mineral needs are a little trickier, since processed food is often lacking these in sufficient quantities. Unless medical reasons dictate otherwise, it is a sensible precaution to use vitamin and mineral supplements. Don't wait until you deplete your energy stores before topping them up; do it on the go, either through solid food or energy drinks (see pp. 102–6).

■ What is your favourite type of riding: hill climbs, time trials, sprinting? What type of riding do you do most? If the two are the same – which they will be for most of us – then that could be another reason for lack of progress. Try to spend 70 per cent of your training time on the weaker aspects of your riding, and 30 per cent on your strong points. The 30 per cent will maintain your strengths and the 70 per cent will improve your weaknesses. If you have reached your plateau through a steady diet of interval training, then go back to basics with a period of sustained continuous rides – or vice versa. Give your body a shock and force it to adapt to some new stresses.

So far, the problems discussed have involved physical, rather than psychological, barriers to improvement. The latter can, however, be as acute as the former. Perhaps you simply don't think that you will ever get fitter. Prove it then! Give yourself 10 weeks to prove that you'll never get better. Start by getting some measure of your current fitness, say a 10-mile time trial. Then sit down, go through the likely reasons for not having improved in the past, and get down to some serious effort on your bike. (Remember to rest effectively too.) After the 10 weeks, re-run your time trial and marvel at the improvement. In all training it is important to set goals that are attainable, given effort. Breaking through a plateau can be done by simply taking a fresh approach to your training and adding some new challenges.

Fitness gains without 'training'

It may seem strange that a book on cycling for fitness, written by a cycling coach, could suggest that you can get fit without following a training plan. However, there are many cyclists who want to get fitter through regular riding, but who don't want to plan and implement a specific schedule. The good news is that you can get fitter without training. In reality, this means getting fitter without actually thinking that you have been training. You will be stressing the body and following the principles of training, but in a more relaxed and subtle way than someone who plans things well in advance. While the results will not be optimal, you will still see gains in fitness and as a result you should gain additional pleasure from your cycling, without ever getting too serious.

The following methods of subtle training will help advance your fitness and require only simple adjustments to the cycling which you are already doing.

How to improve your fitness without a 'training plan'

- Detour. If you normally ride over a similar route take two detours on each ride. This will add to the duration of the rides, which is one of the components of training overload.

- Ride your normal routes in reverse. By doing this not only will you get a new perspective on the scenery, but you will probably have a harder ride – increasing the intensity of the ride, another component of training overload.

- 'Out and back'. Ride away from home for a set time, say 30 minutes, then simply turn around and try to get home in less than 30 minutes. You will be surprised how intense even the most laid-back cyclists become when there is a deadline to beat!

- Speed burst. Decide to ride much faster than normal until the next red car, next large rock, next farmhouse, next whatever – or until you tire; whichever is first.

- The double. Decide that you are going to ride twice as far as your normal route, just to see if you can do it. Don't try to ride very fast, just aim to complete the distance in however long it takes.

- Up a gear. You're riding along in your fourth highest gear. Simply shift on to the next highest, and hold the same pedalling speed for as long as you can.

- Hard hill, easy hill. Decide to ride hard up all the hills. When it's flat or downhill go extra easily, but when the route points upwards – go for it. The next ride, do the opposite: easy on the hills, and as hard as you can sustain on the flat sections.

- A hell week. This is just what it sounds like. For one week, do most of the above. Get yourself well and truly tired and worn out! Then, over the following week, take it easy. Such a hard week will not do any long-term harm, and it comprises a high volume of training stress so that given the easy week which follows, your body will adapt and become stronger and more efficient. Consider it your own little Tour de France!

Total body fitness – 'cross training'

Although cycling is a highly effective form of aerobic exercise, there are certain aspects of fitness that riding alone cannot fully address. Flexibility – or the ability to move joints, and use muscles, through their full range of movement – is one such element and is discussed in relation to 'stretching' in the following chapter.

Another element is upper body strength. While mountain biking over extreme terrain will aid its development to a certain degree, the fact is that cycling is primarily a lower-body activity involving mainly the thighs in a rather limited range of movement. For those wishing to gain what could be referred to as 'total body fitness', it is necessary to incorporate other exercise activities (for example, swimming, rowing, etc) into the weekly cycle training programme. This is sometimes termed 'cross training'.

Some believe that cross training can help achieve a more balanced fitness, which may in itself benefit riding performance and for the purposes of enhancing all-round, 'health-related' fitness for the novice or relative newcomer, cross training can be both effective and highly enjoyable.

Whatever activities you choose, there are two ways of incorporating them into your overall fitness plan. You can either work out an overall cycle training programme as discussed earlier in this chapter, and replace one

'Cycling to work saves me money and means that I know exactly how long my journey will take. I arrive feeling refreshed, positive, virtuous and fitter!'

Charlie, a cyclist for 6 years

or two riding sessions with alternative activities, or you can add the extra activities to your programme (in effect training for cycle fitness without compromise but building in extra sessions to enhance your overall fitness). Of course, the second option requires greater commitment in terms of time and effort, and care should be taken not to over-exercise.

Body conditioning exercises

If you prefer to remain a committed cyclist and have no desire to participate in other sports activities, there is one convenient option available to you. A resistance training programme, comprising two or three 20-minute sessions each week, can be highly effective. By keeping the sessions short, there will be minimal impact on your cycle-specific sessions – indeed, they could be scheduled to form part of your pre-ride warm-up or post-ride cool-down. You don't even need access to a gym; many exercises rely on body-weight and the use of everyday objects – such as filled water bottles – to provide resistance. (For ease of reference, these will be called 'weights' in the exercise descriptions below and are shown as dumbbells.)

It is not within the scope of this book to discuss in full detail the principles and techniques of resistance training, but the following plan would represent a good base for riders seeking all-round muscular conditioning. Your normal riding will provide sufficient conditioning of the legs and buttocks, so this plan focuses on the upper body – the muscles of the arms, shoulders, chest, and abdomen. The most effective means of developing 'whole-body' fitness is through the use of equipment which challenges the ability to balance and co-ordinate movements whilst working against resistance. Such methods are covered in detail in *The Complete Guide to Core Stability* by Matt Lawrence (A & C Black). At the very least, you should aim to use 'free-weights' rather than fixed machine weights thus ensuring some positive involvement of adjacent muscles to stabilise the body in the correct position to undertake the movement.

Some upper-body conditioning exercises

The arms – biceps

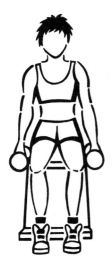 

Positioning

Stand, or sit in a sturdy, stable, arm-less chair. With your feet shoulder-width apart, arms fully extended downwards, hold a weight in each hand, palms facing inwards towards your body.

The exercise ('biceps curl')

Bending the arm at the elbow, lift the weight almost to the shoulder, slowly and smoothly. While lifting, rotate the palm so that it is facing the shoulder at the top of the movement. Slowly return to your side, and repeat. To save time the exercise can be done lifting both arms at the same time, but remember to maintain the correct technique.

67

The arms – triceps

Positioning

Hold a weight in one hand. Bend forwards from the waist until your chest is parallel to the floor, placing your other hand and knee on a bench for stability. Your back should be flat and horizontal. Then bend the arm holding the weight 90 degrees at the elbow, and bring it up so that the upper arm is parallel to and close to the side of your body. The weight should be hanging straight down below the elbow.

The exercise
('triceps kickback')

Keeping your elbow still, extend your arm backwards until it is straight and horizontal. Hold for a count of two, then slowly return to the starting position. Repeat. Make sure that you don't swing the weight, and that you keep your upper arm fixed and your lower back flat and still. Use a relatively light weight until you are confident in your technique. Repeat on the other side.

The arms and shoulders – triceps and deltoids

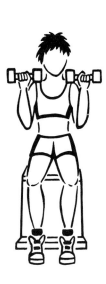 

Positioning

Sit on an upright bench or suitable chair, angled at about 90 degrees, so that your lower back is firmly in contact with it. Hold a weight in each hand, hands facing forwards and level with your shoulders.

The exercise ('shoulder press')

Press the weights directly upwards over your head. As you straighten your arms, make sure that you don't lock your elbows – they should be 'loosely straight'. Lower the weights slowly back to the starting position and repeat.

The shoulders – deltoids

Positioning
Stand with feet hip-width apart. Hold a weight in each hand. Bend forwards slightly and bring the weights in front of your thighs – the hands should be facing each other.

The exercise ('lateral raise')
Raise the weights out to the sides. At the same time, turn your hands so that they face the floor. Raise the weights until your elbows and hands are level with your shoulders. Slowly return to the start position, continuing to resist the weight on the way back down.

The abdominals – rectus abdominis (upper part)

Hands on thighs

Hands across chest

Hands on side of head

Positioning

Lie on the floor, knees bent and feet flat on the floor, hip-width apart. Place your hands on your thighs. Make sure your back isn't 'hollow'; there should be a small gap between your lower back and the floor.

The exercise ('curl-ups')

Breathe in. Then, as you breathe out, pull your abdomen in and slowly round your spine forwards. Lift your head, shoulders and upper back off the floor. Hold for a count of two, then slowly lower to the ground. Repeat.

As an alternative you may wish to use the other positions – hands across chest, or hands on side of head.

The abdominals – obliques
(these wrap diagonally around the waist)

Positioning

Lie on your right side with your knees slightly bent. Place your left arm behind your head.

The exercise
('lying side bends')

Raise your head and shoulders slightly off the floor, breathing out as you do so. You should be 'aiming' your ribs at your top hip. Hold this position for a count of two, then breathe in as you return slowly to the starting position. Repeat on your left side.

The back – spinal extensors

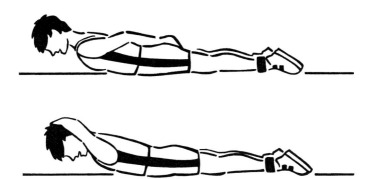

Positioning

Lie face down on the floor, with your hands either on your buttocks, or by the sides of your head, with your elbows out to the sides.

The exercise ('back extensions' or 'hyperextension')

Raise your head, shoulders and upper chest slowly from the floor. (Do not raise more than 12 cm from the floor.) Hold for a count of two and then lower gently back. Make sure you keep your legs relaxed on the floor, and only raise as far as is comfortable.

The chest – pectorals

Positioning

Lie flat on a bench, holding a weight with palms facing forwards and arms fully extended – positioned directly over your chest.

The exercise
('bench or chest press')

Slowly lower the weight down to the armpit area. Hold for a moment, then press the weights smoothly back to the starting position.

Planning your session – some useful tips

For the first session, take each exercise in turn and do as many repetitions as you can – always maintaining the correct technique. For example, say you can do 30 shoulder presses. Then work out what 80 per cent of this maximum is: 30 x 0.8 = 24 repetitions. Using this figure for each exercise, start your resistance training programme. Try to select a weight or resistance that will allow a maximum of 20–30 repetitions for each exercise. This will ensure that your session will develop strength and muscle tone.

Work through each exercise, doing the correct number of repetitions for your 80 per cent figures. When you have done each of the exercises you have completed a full 'set'. Rest for five minutes then do another set. If you feel comfortable, rest for another five minutes, and do a third. This would complete your session.

Remember to re-test yourself every four weeks or so, and recalculate your 80 per cent figures again so that you can maintain sufficient training stress on the muscles. Failure to do this will mean that muscle fitness will be maintained at the level you reach in 4–6 weeks after starting, rather than further enhanced as time goes on. Progression can be achieved through a variety of ways:

- a gradual increase in the number of repetitions using the same weight
- the same number of repetitions using a heavier weight
- for maximum training effect, an increase in repetitions using a heavier weight.

Within just a few months, you will notice that your upper body will be much better toned and your muscles should tire much less easily when cycling.

Know your body

One of the keys to successful training is knowing your body – how it reacts to certain types of training, its optimal diet, when to train and when to have a break, and so on. Generally speaking, it takes athletes a few years to develop an intimate knowledge of their body. They learn to sense the condition of their muscles, to assess how much sleep they need, to decide whether or not their diet is good enough. You must do the same. Look out for signs of overtraining such as insomnia, loss of appetite, loss of enthusiasm and irritability. Some mornings you will be able to tell if a hard ride is possible just by the feeling in your legs while you are still in bed.

Learning what your body is saying is one thing; doing what it says is another. If you feel lousy, why ride? If you feel great, replace a planned easy ride with a hard interval training session. Don't be a slave to your training plan – learn to be flexible. The progressive cycle of stress, recovery and adaptation is not fixed to any timescale you'll read in this or any other book. It will take time and experience to learn when you have recovered.

Over-training

The feeling of fatigue that follows a good ride or workout tells you that you are pushing your physical limits, and this is a necessary part of improving personal performance. However, in certain circumstances, fatigue may also be the only warning that you are pushing too hard and need to 'back off' or risk deterioration in performance – or even illness.

The challenge for you when building your personal training programme is to find your own limits, to separate over-reaching and overtraining. Here's how to tell if you may be exercising too much:

- you wake up in the morning and you feel you have not slept enough, even though you may have had seven to eight hours of uninterrupted sleep
- you lose interest in social activities and sex

- you are short-tempered and irritable, get distracted, and lack patience in your day-to-day activities
- you feel like you need coffee or some other stimulant to give you the energy to get through your next workout
- you wonder if it is all worth it to feel this way

If you feel that your exercise habits could be out of hand, talk to someone you feel comfortable with, such as your doctor, a family member or friend, a professional counsellor, or someone from your social group. Keep in mind that too much exercise does not necessarily make you look better or get stronger. In some cases it can 'flatten out' your muscles and make you more susceptible to injuries and illness.

6 Rest and recovery

Most training programmes include at least one (and sometimes two) rest days per week, as well as a day or two of easy spinning. Over-reaching is a normal part of the training cycle, but if your performance is not improving after a few

> The best cycle rides are the ones where you don't really plan your route beforehand. Getting lost on a trail is always fun, especially if you discover a nice country pub around the corner!
>
> *Robert, a cyclist for 20 years*

days of recovery, it's time to switch to other aerobic activities which will keep you within your training zone.

How long do you need to rest? Studies have indicated that recovery from over-reaching (and again, this means keeping your general level of aerobic activity at around 70 per cent max, not complete inactivity) may take up to two weeks with performance improving daily. As in all aspects of personal training, there is individual variability; so it is up to you to decide where to draw your own line. But remember that rest is a key part of any training programme and may be the most important choice you'll have to make.

Finally, don't forget to pay particular attention to post-exercise carbohydrate replacement. Part of the fatigue of overtraining may be related to chronically inadequate muscle glycogen stores from poor post-training-ride dietary habits.

General considerations

Stretching and massage help you adapt to the rigours of cycling. In addition to enabling a faster recovery and lessening the chances of injury, stretching can also help you to produce more power from your muscles. Since stretching improves flexibility and increases range of motion, well-exercised muscles and joints will undergo less severe stress in extreme training conditions. The longer muscles and joints can perform without failure under stress, the longer you can cycle at your optimum speed. The stiffness and tightness frequently felt after a ride can be brought under control, and even eliminated, with proper stretching after a long or intensive training session or race.

The key muscle groups for a cyclist to work on in stretching sessions are those most used. Crucial is the hamstring, or back of the thigh, since any tightness there may transfer tension to the knees or lower back. Then follow the quadriceps (front of the thigh); the inner thigh; the hip flexor; the calves (both gastrocnemeus and soleus); the shoulders; the upper and lower back; the triceps; the pectorals; and the neck. See illustration.

A slow, static stretch that allows the muscle to relax gradually is the safest course of action. To get the most out of your stretch, begin the exercise gently and hold it in place. The essence of stretching is to lengthen the muscle only to the point of gentle tension. This is an excellent time to listen to your body; stretching should never cause pain, especially joint pain. If it does, you are stretching too far, and you need to reduce the stretch so that it doesn't hurt (although mild discomfort or a mild pulling sensation is normal).

Warm-up stretches, performed before a training session, should comprise three 'efforts' of 10-second holds per muscle or muscle group. To return muscles to their natural length after your workout, hold the stretch for approximately 20 seconds; do two 'efforts' like this for each muscle or muscle group. This will relax the muscle from the repeated contractions of exercise, thus helping to prevent injury. To actively increase your flexibility, try to follow a pattern of once per day, three days a week, 3 x 20 seconds per muscle or mus-

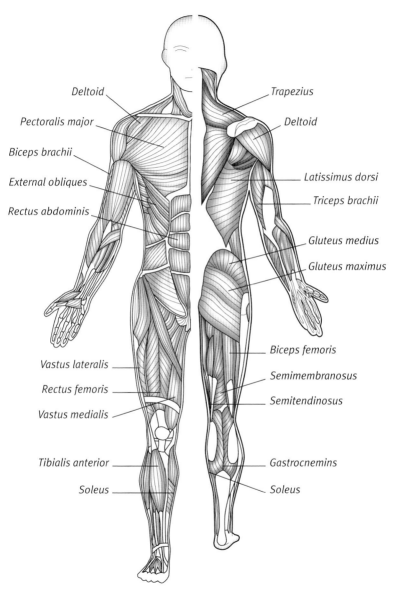

Deltoid

Pectoralis major

Biceps brachii

External obliques

Rectus abdominis

Trapezius

Deltoid

Latissimus dorsi

Triceps brachii

Gluteus medius

Gluteus maximus

Vastus lateralis

Rectus femoris

Vastus medialis

Tibialis anterior

Soleus

Biceps femoris

Semimembranosus

Semitendinosus

Gastrocnemins

Soleus

Major muscle groups used in cycling

cle group, with 20-second rests between stretches. Always remember to stretch only to the point of comfortable tension and stop immediately if you feel any pain in joints or muscles.

When starting a stretch, take a deep breath in and slowly release it as you gradually relax into the stretching position. During the stretch, close your eyes and focus on your breathing. Then, at the point where tension in the muscle begins to release, take another deep breath, filling your lungs and expanding your diaphragm. As you slowly exhale, relax further into the stretch and feel the tension in the muscle melt away.

In addition to stretching during every warm-up and cool-down session, you should include a separate, dedicated stretching session at least once a week. Do a full set of stretches for each part of the body mentioned above. Bear in mind that you need to warm up before these sessions also; a little bit of easy walking or cycling will be sufficient. Never 'bounce' into a stretch; maintain slow, steady movements. Jerking into position can cause muscles to tighten, possibly resulting in injury. Avoid locking your joints into place when you straighten them during stretches – maintain a very slight bend in them.

The stretches

Hamstrings

The muscles in the back of the thigh. These are very important to cycling, since they are active when returning the pedal to the start of the 'power' phase of pedalling.

Positioning

Sit on the floor with your back and shoulders straight. Your right leg should be straight out in front of you, toes pointing up, and your left leg bent out at the side, foot flat on the floor. Your hands can be held behind your back to support the spine, or on the outstretched leg as shown.

Hamstring stretch

The stretch

- Lean forward from your hips (not your waist) until you feel a stretch in your right leg.
- Keep your back and shoulders straight.
- Hold this position for 15–30 seconds.
- Repeat with the other leg, reversing the position.
- Repeat the stretch three to five times on each side.

Quadriceps

The muscles in the front of the thigh – the most active muscles used for cycling. They act to straighten a leg bent at the knee, which, for the cyclist, results in the pedals being pushed down powerfully.

Positioning

Lie on your right side, on the floor. Your hips should be aligned so that the left one is directly above the right one. Ensure that your lower back is not hollowed. Rest your head on a pillow or your right hand. Bend your left knee, reach back with your left hand, and hold on to your left heel as shown. If you can't reach your heel with your hand, loop a belt over your left foot.

Front of thigh quadriceps stretch (lying)

The stretch

- Pull slightly on your foot (with your hand or with the belt) until the front of your right thigh feels stretched.
- Hold this position for 15–30 seconds.
- Reverse your position and repeat with the other leg.
- Repeat the stretch three to five times on each side.
- If the back of your thigh cramps during this exercise, stretch your leg out and try again, more slowly.

Calf muscles – gastrocnemeus

The calf muscles are important for cycling, since they maintain the rigidity of the foot on the pedal, and aid in the final phase of the pedal stroke by pushing the toes downwards.

Positioning

While standing, place your hands on a wall with your arms bent slightly at the elbow. Keep your right knee slightly bent with the toes of your left foot turned inwards slightly – this places emphasis on the gastrocnemus muscle. Move your left foot back one or two feet. Your left heel should be flat on the floor.

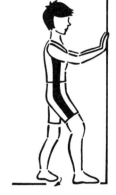

The stretch

- The position should initiate a stretch in your left calf muscle. This shouldn't feel uncomfortable.
- If you don't feel a stretch, move your left foot further back until you do.
- Hold this position for 15–30 seconds.
- Repeat with opposite leg, then again, three to five times on each side.

Calf stretch – gastroenemeus

Calf muscles – soleus

Positioning

As for gastrocnemeus, above, except keep foot in line – don't turn it inwards. This places more emphasis on the soleus.

The stretch

- Keeping your right heel and foot on the floor, bend your right knee slightly.
- Repeat with opposite leg; do the stretch three to five times on each side.

Calf stretch – soleus

The shoulders

The muscles found in the shoulders are used to stabilise riding position, and allow control of the bike steering.

Positioning

Lie on the floor with a pillow under your head, legs straight. (If your back bothers you, you can place a rolled towel under your knees.) Stretch your arms straight out to the side, on the floor. Your upper arms will remain on the floor throughout this exercise. Bend your arms at the elbow so that your hands are pointing towards the ceiling.

Shoulder stretch

The stretch

■ Let your arms roll backwards slowly from the elbow. Stop when you feel a stretch or slight discomfort, and stop immediately if you feel a pinching sensation or a sharp pain.

■ Slowly raise your arms, still bent at the elbow, to point towards the ceiling again.

■ Then let your arms slowly roll forwards, remaining bent at the elbow, to point towards your hips. Again, stop when you feel a stretch or slight discomfort.

■ Alternate these movements, beginning and ending with the 'pointing-above-the-head' position.

■ Hold each position for 15–30 seconds, keeping your shoulders flat on the floor throughout.

■ Repeat three to five times.

Hip flexors

The hip flexors are the primary muscles use in the recovery phase of the pedal stroke, pulling the pedal back to the top position.

Positioning

Begin half kneeling, with your right leg in front. Tighten your abdominal muscles, so that your trunk is stabilised. Alternatively, you can support yourself with one hand on a stool.

Hip flexors (half lunge)

The stretch

- Press your right leg forwards, forcing your left hip into extension.
- Repeat on the other side with your left leg in front.

Hip adductors

These muscles are important for positioning the body especially when riding off-road on technical trails. They also stabilise the legs as they travel through the normal pedalling action.

Positioning

Standing sideways on to a waist-high object, place your right foot up on it. For stability, you can hold on to something throughout the movement.

Hip adductors

The stretch

- Ensure that your toes are pointing forwards.
- Laterally flex your trunk towards the right side (as indicated by arrow).
- Your upper arm must reach towards your foot – not press downwards on the outside of the knee, because this can stress the joint.

Lower back

The lower back muscles are used primarily to stabilise the lower body in the saddle, and they also function as shock absorbers during off-road cycling.

Positioning

Lie on the floor with your knees drawn up to your chest.

The stretch

- Grip your knees.

Lower back

- Pull them into your chest and up towards your shoulders. This should create a 'rocking' movement in the lower spine. To achieve the correct stretch, make sure that you pull the knees to the shoulders and not simply the chest.

Upper back (rhomboids and thoracic spine)

The upper back muscles aid positioning on the bike which is important for clear vision and bike control.

Positioning

Sit on a bench or chair with both arms across your chest. Place your hands on your shoulders.

The stretch

- With both hands firmly on your shoulders, perform a 'flexing' movement to stretch the thoracic spine.

- Be careful not to over-stretch, since this area is often too flexible ('hyper-flexible').

Upper back

Triceps

The triceps are responsible for support-
ing the weight of the upper body on the
handlebars, and for pulling on the handlebars when lifting out of the saddle.

Positioning

Stand with your feet hip-width apart,
with your left hand over your left shoulder in the centre of your back. Place
your right hand at your left elbow.

The stretch

Triceps

- Use your right hand to ease your left
  arm further back, using a gentle pressure on the left elbow.
- Repeat on the other side.
- Ensure that you keep your knee joints loosely straight, and don't
  hollow your lower back.
- Stretch only to a point where gentle tension is felt at the back of
  your upper arm.

Pectorals

These muscles are used primarily for upper body
support. You will use them more when taking
part in off-road cycling events.

Positioning

Stand with your feet hip-width apart, arms down
by your sides.

The stretch

- Take your hands backwards slowly, keeping
  your arms loosely straight, until you feel a
  stretch at the front of your chest.
- You can place your hands on your buttocks, or
  clasp them together behind your back,
  depending on comfort.

Pectorals

Massage

The primary aim of massage is to aid recovery by stimulating blood flow through the muscles. This drains away the toxic by-products of exercise, and helps to re-align tangled or knotted muscle fibres. Because the technique is always to rub towards the heart, massage replicates the pumping action of active muscles which 'shunt' blood back to the heart through one-way valves in the veins.

It's worth giving massage a go, even if you're inexperienced. If nothing else, a good rub will help you to relax after a hard ride – as long as you don't dig too deep into sore muscle.

Massage technique

- Start with the front of the thigh, using the thumb and fingers to gently massage each muscle.
- The circulation through the knee can be stimulated using the thumbs in a circular motion, slowly working around the edge of the kneecap. Be careful not to dig too deep into the joint.
- Move on to the shin, stroking the muscles on either side of the shin-bone upwards towards the knee.
- Rubbing hard from side to side across the calf muscles, rather than along the length of them, helps to loosen them prior to stroking actions later in the massage.
- Move on to the back of the thigh, rubbing gently from the knee to the hip.
- Try a 'kneading' action, followed by stroking.
- Move back to the calves again, using the fingers to smooth out the muscle, and running the palm of the hands down the length of the muscles.
- Gentle 'kneading' by the thumb and forefinger on the Achilles tendon increases blood flow through the tendon, which is usually much less than the blood flow through muscle.
- Finish off using flushing strokes along the full length of the legs, back then front.

7 Fuel for fitness

It may seem that many cyclists have an unusually close relationship with food. If you take the right approach to what and how much you eat, you can see dramatic improvements in your health and performance – even without changing your training habits.

The nutrients that we gain from food perform several functions: energy provision; tissue building and repair; and regulation of the body's functions – carbohydrates give energy, proteins are largely responsible for building and repairing tissue, and fat supports vital organs and acts as an energy reserve. No nutrient acts independently of the others: they must all be present in your body for you to function well. You should eat a wide variety of healthy foods: variety and balance are the keys to a healthy diet. The six essential dietary components are water, protein, carbohydrate, fat, vitamins and minerals.

Water

The condition of the body, its performance, and its ability to resist injury is to a great extent dependent on adequate fluid intake. Dehydration occurs when you do not drink enough fluid to replace all that lost through perspiration, respiration, urination and other body processes. Approximately 3 litres are lost each day under normal conditions, and during prolonged exercise, 1–2 litres of water an hour can be eliminated through sweating. There is no built-in alarm clock within the body that tells you when dehydration is taking place. Thirst is not a sufficient indicator, since you can feel thirsty in a state of adequate hydration. When you are dehydrated, your blood is more 'concentrated' and less able to deliver oxygen to the brain and muscles; cooling of the body, through sweating, cannot take place. The digestive system is less efficient and the joints of the body are not properly lubricated.

Body fluid can be replaced via any drink including milk, fruit juices and vegetable juices, and through many of the foods we eat. However, plain water is best. Coffee and tea are poor choices because they act as diuretics, stimulating further water loss. Cold water is absorbed faster than room temperature water, leading to faster fuel delivery. It also supplies a reservoir of cold in the stomach that absorbs body heat. Later in this chapter the role of fluid intake before, during and after training will be explored. At these times optimal hydration can make the difference between riding for fitness and simply riding.

Protein

Protein makes up the second largest part of the body, after water. Protein is the major source of building material for internal organs, muscle, blood, skin, hair and nails. Protein is also needed for the formation of hormones, enzymes, and antibodies. Every cell in the body contains some protein.

The body continues to repair itself 24 hours a day. This requires protein to be in the bloodstream at all times for optimum health. A complete protein consists of 22 'building blocks' known as 'amino acids'. Eight of these are considered 'essential amino acids'. If any one of these eight is not in the foods you eat, your body will suffer from a protein deficiency and it will 'cannibalise' itself by burning protein stored in the muscles to protect the heart, kidneys and other vital organs. Such is its importance in the diet that, unlike carbohydrates and fats, you could live on protein alone. You can burn all three for fuel, but only protein can also be used for muscular growth and repair.

Proteins containing all of the eight essential amino acids can be found in both animals and plants. One source is no better than another. Good sources of protein are meat, cheese, milk, fish and eggs, as well as beans, peas and soya beans. Vegetable proteins such as lentils, dried beans, peas, nuts and cereals are considered 'incomplete' proteins because one or more of the essential amino acids is missing; only by combining several of them at the same time will you get a complete protein. Remember that many protein-rich sources are also high in saturated fat (see p. 106), so try to get as much of your protein from vegetables, fish and white meat, with lean cuts of red meat and reduced fat dairy produce as second choice.

> I ride off-road fairly regulary with a friend. It's a great way to escape the normal routine, good fun and often very challenging. It is also something that I don't need to travel very far to do.
>
> *Grant, cyclist for 18 years*

Those involved in heavy exercise or hard manual labour need more protein each day than a relatively sedentary person; as a general rule the recommended protein intake for regular exercisers ranges from 1 gram to 1.5 grams per kilogram of body weight. So a 70 kg cyclist should aim to consume 70 to 105 grams of protein daily. As there are 4 calories to 1 gram of protein, this equates to 280–420 calories. As the body can break down fats and carbohydrates faster than protein as a fuel for the body, protein is not normally used as a fuel supply unless insufficient fats and carbohydrates are present in the diet.

Carbohydrates

Carbohydrates are the major dietary energy source for most adults, providing fuel for muscle activity and brain function. They yield 4 kilocalories of energy per gram, the same as protein (fat yields 9 kcal/g), and between 40% and 60% of the daily energy 'replacement' calories in a typical 'western' diet. The body will burn protein and fat as energy fuel when necessary, but – due in part to ease of digestion – 'prefers' carbohydrates, especially at the exercise intensities most common to general fitness training.

Carbohydrates can be divided into two types: 'simple' carbohydrates, such as table, fruit and milk sugars, and 'complex' carbohydrates (such as starch), which are found in potatoes, brown rice, dried beans, fresh fruits and vegetables, and wholegrain breads and cereals. Simple carbohydrates are broken down very quickly; complex ones are broken down more slowly so that limited amounts of glucose are in the bloodstream at any one time.

Any excess glucose is stored in the liver and muscles as glycogen and is available for future energy needs. However, the body can only store a limited amount, around 1600–2000 kcal – enough to last an average person roughly one day if they were to eat nothing.

Research suggests that 60–65 per cent of your total daily calorific intake should come from carbohydrates. Complex carbohydrates should make up the majority of the carbohydrate requirement. As well as providing a good nutritional 'package', these foods also contain dietary fibre, an important element in regulating bowel function.

The amount of carbohydrate that you should eat daily is closely linked to the number of calories you need to take in each day in order to maintain your weight. As a rough guide, active women require between 1600 and 2200 calories daily; active men need between 2800 and 3200 calories a day. It is advisable for women to aim for 6 to 9 servings from the bread group, 3 to 4 servings from the vegetable group, and 2 to 3 servings from the fruit group daily. Active men can eat around 11 servings from the bread group; 5 from the vegetable group, and 4 from the fruit group. Both men and women should have up to 3 daily servings from the milk group – another good source of carbohydrates (see p. 98, the food pyramid).

Fats

Body fat and body composition

The body is made up of two elements: 'lean body tissue', which includes muscle, bone and blood; and 'body fat' (sometimes called adipose tissue). The proportion of the two elements within the body is known as body composition.

There are three main types of body fat.

■ Essential fat. This is vital for survival. It includes the fat surrounding organs such as the heart and kidneys, which insulates and protects them from damage; and the fat which helps to make up cell membranes, the brain and bone marrow

■ Sex-specific fat. In women, this is stored mainly in the breasts and around the hips, and ensures normal hormone balance and menstruation. In men it is stored mainly around the waist

■ Storage fat, which is an important energy reserve providing 9 kcal/g – over twice as much as both carbohydrate and protein. Of the three fuel sources, fat is the most economical so that during long day tours, ridden at a relatively low intensity, it will be a major energy provider. It is most commonly used as fuel when the intensity is below 50 per cent maximum aerobic capacity.

As well as being an important energy source, the third type of fat is the one which most people worry about. Present in excess, it forms a potentially serious health risk. A healthy body fat percentage is around 13–18 per cent for men and 18–25 per cent for women. There are several different ways in which body fat can be measured; the most simple is by skinfold measurement using callipers. Most health clubs and sports centres use this method.

It is important to remember that very low body fat levels can be harmful too, increasing the risk of respiratory disease, certain cancers and metabolic disorders. A minimum body fat percentage of 5 per cent for men and 10% for women is generally considered necessary for basic body function.

Dietary fat

Any excess calories taken into the body are converted into fat. Therefore, it is a general truth that the percentage of fat present in your body is linked directly to your diet.

Dietary fats and oils consist mainly of triglycerides, composed of a unit of glycerol and three fatty acids. These fatty acids are classified into two main types, according to their chemical structure: 'saturated' and 'unsaturated'. Of these, the saturated fatty acids are most detrimental to health, since they can increase harmful blood cholesterol levels and thus increase the risk of heart disease. They are found mainly in animal products such as butter, cheese and meat fat. Unsaturated fats, found mainly in plants and fish, should therefore make up the majority of your fat intake.

In terms of your fat intake, for the purposes of cycling for fitness, you should have a balanced and varied diet. If the main aim of your fitness programme is to reduce body fat, a programme of regular aerobic exercise combined with good nutrition should be sufficient for you to see significant progress in a relatively short time (see also pp. 98–100, the food pyramid, and p. 101, a sample daily diet). At elite levels it becomes necessary to follow a stricter regime; see Chapter 8.

Vitamins

Vitamins act as catalysts for the metabolic processes that convert fats, carbohydrates and proteins into calories – or energy. Many of the processes which take place in the body during and after exercise are facilitated by vitamins: for example, vitamin E is a powerful antioxidant, enhancing recovery after hard exercise and literally preventing disease by protecting cells from free radical 'attack' (see p. 99).

If you are concerned about your diet being vitimin deficient, there is no harm in using a simple, over-the-counter multi-vitamin once a day. However, vitamins are not the easy answer to increased health and fitness.

Minerals

Minerals are chemical elements found in the body either in their elemental form or combined with organic compounds. Like vitamins, they are essential for normal cell function. The two most common minerals, calcium and phosphorus, are major components of bone; while sodium and potassium are found in all tissue fluids, both within and around cells.

Magnesium, chloride, sulphur and zinc are other minerals that play a key role in cell function. The trace elements iron, manganese, copper and iodine are found in much smaller quantities, but play essential roles in facilitating basic cellular chemical processes.

In terms of supplementing, the same applies as for vitamins above. Given the fact that modern production methods may adversely affect the content and quality of nutrients present in food, it may well be wise to take a quality supplement as a 'safety net' – unless, of course, you have any medical condition that dictates against it.

Eating to maximise health

Eating more healthily doesn't need to be difficult. A useful means of establishing your daily dietary needs is by using the food pyramid. This provides a graphic guide for making healthy food choices. The pyramid calls for eating a variety of foods to get the nutrients you need, while eating the right amount of calories to maintain a healthy body weight. Each of the pyramid food groups provides some, but not all, of the nutrients you need. Foods in one group cannot replace those from another. No one food group is more important than any other, but for a balanced diet, those foods at the top should be consumed more sparingly than those at the base.

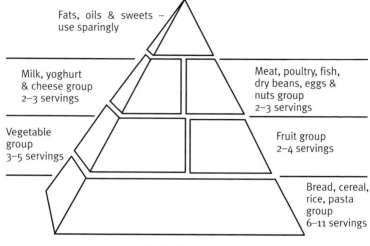

The food pyramid

The top of the pyramid

Fats, oils and sugar should be eaten sparingly and therefore are represented as the small tip of the pyramid. They are present in salad dressings, oils, cream, butter, margarine, soft drinks, candies and sweet desserts; they provide calories but few or no vitamins and minerals.

The middle of the pyramid

Protein is needed in moderate amounts and therefore represents the upper middle of the pyramid. Milk, yoghurt, cheese, meat, poultry, fish, dry beans, eggs and nuts are important sources of protein as well as good sources of calcium, iron and zinc. Choose lean meats, skinless poultry, fish and low-fat dairy products to control fat and cholesterol intake. Also, limit breaded or fried foods for the same reason.

Fruit and vegetables can be regarded as helping to form the 'foundation' of the pyramid. Besides being an excellent source of vitamins, minerals and fibre, these plant foods are low in fat and sodium, and are free of cholesterol. Eating a variety of vegetables and fruits will help ensure that you meet your daily vitamin C requirement – 40 mg per day for men and women – and other nutrients. You should aim to eat five or more servings of fruits and vegetables every day. The following all equate to one serving (the 'cup' measurement is used for simplicity – there is no need to get out the kitchen scales to eat healthily, simply scoop or pour out a cupful as a guide).

- 1 medium fruit or $\frac{1}{2}$ cup of small or cut-up fruit
- $\frac{3}{4}$ cup of 100 per cent fruit juice
- $\frac{1}{4}$ cup dried fruit
- $\frac{1}{2}$ cup raw or cooked vegetables
- 1 cup raw leafy vegetables (e.g. lettuce, spinach)
- $\frac{1}{2}$ cup cooked beans or peas (e.g. lentils, pinto beans, kidney beans)

Research indicates that people who eat lots of fruit and vegetables may be less at risk from cancer than those who don't. This may be due to their relatively high content of 'antioxidants'. These help the body to deal with, and prevent the excessive formation of, free radicals in our system. Free radicals can be described as molecules that have gone 'awry' as a result of oxidised or 'bad' oxygen. They are reactive chemicals capable of randomly damaging DNA and proteins. Exercise that is sufficiently hard to elicit a training response will result in some degree of free radical formation. Vitamins A, C and E form a powerful antioxidant group, and the trace minerals selenium and zinc also play a key antioxidant role.

The base of the pyramid

Bread, cereals, rice and pasta – all foods from grains – are found at the base of the pyramid because they are the foundation upon which the rest of the diet is planned. Try to choose 6–11 servings daily. Grains supply fibre, carbohydrates, vitamins and minerals. They are usually low in fat, and are the preferred fuel for our brain, nervous system and muscles. The cyclist who is training regularly will obviously need to be taking in more calories than a relatively sedentary person, but also needs to increase the consumption of essential endurance-related nutrients such as complex carbohydrates, as well as iron and essential fats. The complex carbohydrates of greatest benefit are found in pasta, rice, bread and grains, as well as potatoes from the middle of the pyramid. Try always to go for wholegrain varieties where possible, since these are an important aid to digestion.

What counts as one serving?

Here are some examples of serving size for each food group. If you eat a larger portion, count it as more than one serving. Try to eat at least the lowest number of servings from the five food groups each day (again, the cup is used as the simplest means of measurement).

Bread, cereal, rice and pasta group (6–11 servings)

- 1 slice of bread
- 1 ounce of ready-to-eat cereal (check labels: 1 ounce = $^1/_4$ cup to 2 cups depending on cereal)
- $^1/_2$ cup of cooked cereal, rice or pasta
- $^1/_2$ hamburger roll, bagel, wholemeal scone
- 3 or 4 plain crackers (small)

Vegetable group (3–5 servings)

- 1 cup of raw leafy vegetables
- $^1/_2$ cup of other vegetables, cooked or chopped raw
- $^3/_4$ cup of vegetable juice

Fruit group (2–4 servings)

- 1 medium apple, banana, orange, nectarine or peach
- $^1/_2$ cup of chopped, cooked or canned fruit
- $^3/_4$ cup of fruit juice

Milk, yoghurt and cheese group (2–3 servings)

- 1 cup of milk or yoghurt
- $1^1/_2$ ounces of natural cheese
- 2 ounces of processed cheese

Meat, poultry, fish, dry beans, eggs, and nuts group (2–3 servings)

- 2–3 ounces of cooked, lean meat, poultry, or fish (1 ounce of meat is equivalent to $\frac{1}{2}$ cup of cooked dry beans, one egg or two tablespoons of peanut butter).

Sample daily diet for a cyclist in training

The following sample meals are intended to give you an idea of the correct variety and quantity of food required by a cyclist undertaking regular training. They are not intended to be followed strictly, and may not give you the total calorie intake that you need.

Breakfast	1 cup bran cereal 1 banana 1 tsp margarine 500 ml low-fat milk 1 slice wholemeal bread 250 ml fruit juice
Lunch	150 grams lean meat 2 tsp mayonnaise or mustard $\frac{1}{2}$ cup coleslaw Lettuce and tomato 1 bread roll 2 oatmeal cookies 1 fresh peach 500 ml water
Dinner	Chicken stir-fry: 1 cup diced vegetables 2 cups rice 1 cup yoghurt 3 ounces chicken 2 tsp oil 1 cup orange and grapefruit sections 500 ml fruit juice
Snack	3 cups popcorn 500 ml fruit juice

The vegetarian cyclist

A diet rich in carbohydrate may lead many riders to what is essentially a form of vegetarian diet. A major concern about vegetarian diets has always been how to ensure a balanced intake of nutrients. While a lacto-vegetarian or ovolacto-vegetarian diet may meet all nutritional needs, there may be a shortage of iron, calcium, iodine, selenium, zinc, riboflavin, vitamin D and vitamin B12 in a strictly vegetarian diet. Iron intake may also be low in a lacto-vegetarian diet, because of the lack of haeme-iron from meat sources, which is more easily absorbed than iron from vegetable sources; and in fact aids the absorption of iron from vegetable sources.

To get a balanced distribution of essential amino acids, vegetarians must eat foods that possess mutual supplementation of dietary protein. This is a nutritional strategy in which vegetable foods with low contents of amino acids (cereals, for example) are eaten together with a food that is high in that same amino acid (for example, milk or beans). To obtain an intake of good quality proteins in the diet, the following food combinations are recommended:

- pasta with cheese
- rice and milk pudding
- cereals with milk or egg
- potatoes with egg or cheese
- rice and beans
- lentils and bread.

If care is taken to include a wide variety of foods, and to combine them in an appropriate way, vegetarian diets can be nutritionally adequate and will not impair your training.

Nutrition for cycle training

Before a training session, there are three important questions that the cyclist must consider.

- Am I adequately hydrated?

- Have I enough energy available for the session?
- Has my last meal had time to leave the stomach?

For short (i.e. less than one hour), moderate intensity rides, taking in water will be more than adequate. But if you train hard and often, water won't be enough; you will need to take in additional carbohydrates for 'fuel'. Failure to do so may result in your training at less than optimal intensity, and thus a less effective use of your precious training time.

Snacking on solid or liquid food while on the bike is important. However, as intensity increases above 60 per cent, it becomes more important to avoid eating within two hours of the training session to avoid stomach discomfort. If you're going to be doing intervals it is vital to have your stomach empty or you risk stomach distress. You will also sweat more so fluid replacement needs to be carried out with special care. Even though you may be spending less time training when doing intervals, a hard interval session of 30 minutes can leave your glycogen stores depleted, so maintain normal energy drink intake and post-training loading (see below).

After training comes what is known as the 'glycogen window', so post-exercise, your body is much more efficient at replacing the carbohydrate stores which may have been depleted by the training session. Therefore, it is wise to have a carbohydrate snack available immediately after your ride finishes. Eat at least 50 grams of carbohydrate just after exercise, and consume a total of at least 100 grams of carbohydrate in the subsequent 4-hour period. Further carbohydrate intake may be advisable for the next 18 to 20 hours; aim to consume at least 600 grams of carbohydrate during the 24 hours after an intense workout or competition.

A high-carbohydrate diet increases stores of glycogen – the energy for muscles – and improves overall performance. If you exercise for longer than an hour, you can begin to deplete your muscle glycogen stores. By consuming 30 to 75 grams per hour of carbohydrate in liquid or solid form when you exercise, you can minimise this effect. After a long (90 minutes or more) workout or competition, your depleted muscle glycogen stores must be fully replenished, especially if you will be exercising again within the next 12–24 hours.

Hydration for cycle training

You must ensure that you are fully hydrated. As a rule, daily fluid intake (excluding fluids used when riding) should be in the region of 2–3 litres. As a rough guide to ensure optimal hydration levels, 5–6 glasses of water per day should be consumed on top of any other drinks. Because carbohydrate is stored along with water in the muscle, a high carbohydrate intake with low fluid intake can lead to water being drawn from other tissues, leaving you close to dehydration before the session even starts. Proper fluid replacement before, during, and after training improves performance. Maintaining body fluid levels during training becomes especially important when the loss from the skin and expired air exceeds 2 litres per hour, as it often does in hot weather.

> Riding together as a family is a good way to spend some quality time together. I am just in the process of teaching my two girls to cycle, and there is a huge sense of acievement for all of us when we see how far they have ridden without mum or dad holding them up!
>
> *Grant, cyclist for 18 years*

Furthermore, hydration with plain water dilutes the blood rapidly and stimulates an increase in urine production – this in turn leads to greater dehydration. Re-hydration will occur more rapidly when drinks containing sodium (salt) – the major electrolyte (the mineral salts dissolved in the body's fluid) lost in sweat – are consumed. A drink containing sodium helps to maintain thirst while delaying the stimulation of urine production. The drink should also ideally contain glucose or sucrose, because these carbohydrates provide an energy source for working muscles, stimulate fluid absorption in the gut, and improve the taste. The following guidelines will help you maintain proper hydration during training and competition.

Energy drinks

An energy drink is especially formulated for the rapid replacement of carbohydrates and electrolytes lost or used up as a result of intensive exercise. Being mostly water, energy drinks are also useful because they rehydrate the body at the same time. In theory, energy drinks are not needed by cyclists riding at a moderate intensity, and for less than 90 to 120 minutes. Your body has adequate energy stores for that amount of time. However, you'll recover your energy more quickly at the end of the ride if you have at least partially replenished those stores en route. Since they are in liquid form, the nutrients in energy drinks begin to enter the bloodstream in as little as 10 to 15 minutes.

Maintaining hydration during training and competition

- Weigh yourself without clothes before and after training and racing, especially during hot weather. For each pound of body weight lost, drink two cups of fluid.
- Use a drink containing sodium to quickly replenish lost body fluids. This drink should also contain 6–8 per cent glucose or sucrose (see above).
- Drink 2.5 cups of fluid two hours before training or competition.
- Drink 1.5 cups of fluid 15 minutes before a session or event.
- Drink at least 1 cup (roughly 2 mouthfuls) of fluid every 15–20 minutes during training and competition.
- Do not restrict your normal fluid intake before or during an event.
- Avoid drinks containing caffeine and alcohol, because they increase urine production and lead to further dehydration.

Energy drinks help to maintain energy and strength, but many of them also have a diuretic effect which can be a nuisance when riding. They also make some riders feel nauseous. Use a drink that you actually like, or you won't drink enough and may get dehydrated. The energy drinks that work best have a concentration of 5–8% sugar for optimal absorption. Fructose can cause stomach upsets and is in any case absorbed slowly. Dextrose and sucrose metabolise more slowly than glucose, but are still relatively quick compared with fructose. Amino acids speed absorption. Sodium and potassium increase water absorption and make the drinks taste better. Today's energy drink market offers a wide choice of flavours and a range of ingredients. For the majority of riders, a basic glucose-polymer based drink is more than adequate and provides a cost-effective means of fuelling training rides.

The following are fine (prices at time of writing): Maxim (£11.95 per 2000 grams); High5 (£12.99 per 1400 grams).

Solid food works just as well to keep up energy levels, but the nutrients can take 30 minutes to reach the bloodstream, so you must plan ahead. Plain water – even with a pinch of salt – works just as well to keep the body hydrated.

Weight loss

Simply put, weight is a matter of balance between calorific intake (in) and expenditure (out). Calorific requirements differ for everyone and are determined by age, sex, weight and level of activity. Body weight will change when there is an imbalance between calories in and calories out. To lose weight, intake must be less than expenditure. In short, to lose weight you must eat less or exercise more, or do a combination of both.

To put weight loss in perspective, use the formula below:

3500 calories ÷ 7 days per week = 500 calories per day

Weight loss is most successful when diet and exercise are combined. Eating 500 calories fewer per day will result in a weight loss of one pound per week. Eating 250 calories less per day combined with a 250-calorie deficit from exercise or training will also result in the same weight loss of one pound per week; however, it will be a healthier, more balanced way of losing weight.

One of the most effective means of achieving fat loss is to utilise interval training. Although interval training is more intensive than most 'fat-burning' exercise programmes, and burns significantly less fat as fuel than more gentle activity it massively increase the calories burned during exercise. In addition, the heat production after exercise has finished is much greater after intervals, there is greater fat burning during recovery and the appetite is reduced post-exercise compared to after steady state training.

8 Cycle sport training

Cycle sport in its many forms demands a high degree of efficiency in the various components of fitness discussed throughout this book. If you have developed good endurance, you will be able to complete almost any form of cycle sport. However, at elite athlete level you will need to move beyond the ability simply to finish an event; you must develop the specific elements of fitness that will allow you to 'compete'– rather than just participate – within a discipline. These fitness elements do not exist in isolation, but rather overlap and interrelate according to the demands of your chosen event.

Cycle sports – the various disciplines

Road racing

Road racing (mass-start events on roads or paved tracks), encompasses events ranging from 50-minute town centre criteriums (usually a course of one mile or less) to one-day classics over 280 km, and ultimately to the three-week-long 4,500 km Tour de France. Within a given race, the power outputs required can vary greatly.

Success in road racing will only come if you have developed sufficient specialist fitness to deal with the many variables which the

Cycle sport training – the requisite fitness element

- Aerobic conditioning. The ability to ride for extended periods at sub-maximal levels; such as during a relatively inactive day spent in the main peloton within a multi-day road stage race, or a 200 km randonnee.

- Aerobic power, or VO2max. The maximum amount of oxygen you can extract from the air and use in the working muscles for the aerobic production of energy. It is particularly relevant to 'high power' endurance work of 3–8 minutes' duration, such as that done by a track rider over a 4000 m pursuit.

- Intensity threshold. The ability to ride at a high percentage of your maximum for sustained periods (more than 20 minutes) without suffering rapid fatigue; for example, during a 40 km time trial.

- Muscular endurance. The ability to sustain repeated muscle contractions at a higher force than is normally required; for example, powering over a short climb in a higher gear than would normally be used.

- Explosive power. The ability to develop near maximal force in a very short time; such as sprinting hard to establish a gap between you and other riders when trying to break away from a group.

- Pain tolerance. The ability to continue a high work rate while suffering pain and discomfort in the propulsive muscles; for example, a track rider sustaining high power for 90 seconds, trying to bridge a 60 m gap in a points race.

event can throw at you. The successful road racer must possess high levels of each element of fitness: base endurance; aerobic power for more intense, sustained efforts such as short climbs; intensity threshold for time trial stages and lone attacks; explosive power for effective springs and attacks; and pain tolerance for occasional forays over the intensity threshold. Muscular endurance needs to be developed to aid riding in strong winds and on gradual, short climbs when high speeds must be maintained. The highly tactical aspect of road racing means that the event is taxing psychologically as well as physically.

Time trials

Time trials require riders to raise their intensity quickly to the 'threshold' level, then attempt to maintain this intensity for the duration of the event. Depending on the length of the event, they may need to work on some specific fitness areas such as pain tolerance or a high aerobic conditioning for 100 mile–24 hour tests.

Effective training will increase the power that can be produced, having made the energy pathways more efficient, increased the blood supply to the muscle (hence aiding removal), and improving the ability of the blood to 'buffer' the effects of high acidity in the muscle, before lactic acid begins to accumulate and fatigue sets in.

Attributes such as explosive power and pain tolerance are less essential for the time trialist, who essentially brings his power output up to his threshold, and seeks to maintain it for the duration of the event. The threshold will vary depending on the length of the test, with sustainable heart rates varying by up to 15 beats for 10-mile compared with 5-mile events.

Mountain bike racing

Mountain bike racing has two main branches – cross-country and downhill. Cross-country racing involves sustained, high intensity riding on rough off-road tracks of between 10 and 40 miles. Although it appears to be an extremely arduous sport, it is in fact one of the easiest and most accessible for the novice. It is open to beginners, with special categories for novices; such rides are carried out over the same terrain as for elite riders, but will be much shorter. Bike-handling skills are important, although you can always get off and push if necessary! There is usually a far less intimidating atmosphere at cross-country than at other events and races, and there are rarely any mountains in sight – even city wasteground and urban parkland have been used for international elite races.

Downhill racing involves high speed descents over steep and technical trails, and is largely a power and strength sport – although there is an endurance element. However, downhill racing does require a great deal of skill; more perhaps than any other branch of cycle sport.

Track racing

The one factor which separates track from other disciplines is the need to develop a high cadence or pedalling speed. This can only be trained by many hours of high-cadence riding. A cyclist who spends a lot of time racing on the track at high speed will often find that when they turn to other disciplines such as road racing, they lack higher-end power and strength. This is because developing high levels of endurance prevents the development of high levels of strength. Relatively light pedal resistance but high pedalling speed trains more endurance-oriented muscle, leading to a decline in the efficiency of strength-oriented muscle.

Planning a race training programme

Planning a race training programme involves the same principles that were examined in Chapter 5. The difference is that specificity in training becomes rather more important for the competitive cyclist. In addition, training must be planned to ensure that you are free from fatigue on the day of the event. The four main steps in planning a race programme are set out below.

Identify the demands of your chosen event

Take your chosen event and consider the following questions.

- How long does the event last?
- Is the intensity consistent or variable?
- If variable, what is the lowest intensity you will be faced with?

- What is the highest intensity you will be faced with?
- How rapid are the changes in intensity?
- What are all the possible scenarios influencing the result? For example, wind direction and strength could be crucial in a road race; technical (bike control) ability could come to the fore when racing off-road in wet weather; or being drawn against an overly aggressive rider may affect tactics in a track sprint.

Identify your weaknesses and strengths

List everything that you feel prevents you from winning. Then, using a scale of 1 to 10 (1 = very poor, 10 = excellent), subjectively evaluate yourself in respect of the six aspects of cycle fitness given below. It's even worth getting some input from other riders – maybe you're not as great a sprinter as you think! The main thing is to be honest. Generally, if you enjoy something you will be good at it; so if you hate climbing, it's likely that you could make some improvements in that area.

Now write down the competitive fitness components where you feel that you are weak (a score of less than 4), and then all those which you feel are your strengths (a score of 8 or more).

Identify your training opportunities

Next, you must consider how much time you have to train each week. Be honest, and don't forget to include the time that it takes to get ready for a ride, to warm up and cool down, and to change and shower afterwards.

Plan your programme

Now that you've worked out when you'll train, and what aspects of fitness you wish to improve, you can start to put it into the larger perspective of races or major rides.

To improve fitness and speed you need to stress the body, allow time for it to adapt to the stress, then stress it again. A potential problem with the need for training overload is the mere fact that the human body is so able to adapt to the stresses imposed upon it during training. For elite cyclists, this can mean increasing training stress levels to such a height that the body's power of recovery simply can't 'keep up'. Training must therefore be redesigned to target weak points, and to focus on one physiological system or structure while another is recovering. For example, when tired from a high-intensity interval training session, a low-intensity continuous ride can often be scheduled the next day without adversely affecting recovery.

Ideally, you want to race after a period of adaptation, since the body's various systems will be recovered and at optimal capacity – energy levels will be high, muscle structures will be repaired and everything will be ready for action. Work your body hard during periods when there are few important races, and ease off to allow adaptation in the lead-up to races. If you have races marked up it's easier, starting a build-up and recovery phase weeks before the race. You can also do this before big day trips and tours. Too many riders train hard right up to a race, do badly, get fed up, stay off the bike for a few days, then get back on and feel 110 per cent. They had their recovery phase after the race, rather than before.

In general, spend 20 per cent of your time working on your strengths and 50 per cent of your time on weaknesses (with 30 per cent on everything else). This should result in improvements in all aspects of your riding, but will specifically aim towards eliminating weaknesses.

Race preparation

Do not make the mistake of trying to train for a race the week before. Race fitness is developed in the weeks before an event. Familiarise yourself with your competitors and the course, and you can alter your training to help you prepare as optimally as time allows. Ideally you should allow three weeks of specific preparation, and spend the week immediately prior to the event recuperating – this is known as a 'taper' week.

When not racing, use your time to work on weaknesses, building up both the intensity and duration of rides. Include some hard efforts on hills, on the flat, sprinting and time trialing. Remember to eat well during periods of intense training, and rest well too. During the taper refine your riding skills. Gradually reduce the training duration, while still keeping intensity relatively high – for instance, go from 25-mile to 10-mile time trials, or do half the usual number of intervals. Then, as race day approaches, ease off completely, still riding but not training. The day before, ride half the race distance, with three or four 1-minute efforts at race pace.

At an event

When you get to an event, you should allow some time to look over the course – either on the bike, if it won't tire you, or in a car. Note the positioning of hills, any difficult descents and corners, and any potholes and storm covers which may cause problems. For road race reconnaissance, check where the best places will be to attack or to recover after an attack, where the wind is likely to be strongest, and on what parts of the course you can get shelter.

Make sure you eat nothing in the two hours before the event, but sip fluids up to the start time. Ensure that you warm up for at least 20, and preferably 30, minutes before the start. An ideal pre-event warm-up might be:

- 20 minutes at 65 per cent max heart rate
- 5 x 10-second maximal sprints, with 50 seconds recovery
- 5 minutes progressing from 60 per cent to 80 per cent max heart rate
- race

Afterwards

Consider what went right or wrong during the race, and why? Where did you lose out, what would you do differently next time, and what can you improve? Be fair and try to stay clear of blaming others. Don't forget to look at things like your diet and sleep patterns in the days leading up to the race; these are often the cause of seem-ingly inexplicable poor performances.

Nutrition for competition

For advice on general nutritional principles, refer to Chapter 7, pp. 91–116.

A few days before a prolonged and intense competitive event, regulate your diet and training to maximise or 'load' muscle glycogen stores. High pre-exercise glycogen levels will allow you to exercise harder for longer by delaying fatigue. The most practical method of glycogen loading involves training intensely to the fifth or sixth day before competition. During the remaining days, you should gradually reduce the amount of training and eat high-carbohydrate meals (more than 600 grams) on each day of the final three days before an event. Such a regimen will increase muscle glycogen stores to 20–40 per cent above normal.

The pre-competition meal

A high-carbohydrate meal eaten within six hours of competition 'tops off' the glycogen stores in both liver and muscle. Even after following a muscle glycogen loading regimen, it is wise to eat a low-fat meal containing 75–150 grams of carbohydrate three hours before competition. Carbohydrate consumption will vary with athletes' energy expenditure and body size. Values given for carbohydrate intake are guidelines for a 70 kg rider; they should be adjusted according to individual cyclists' needs.

Appendix

Avoiding common cycling ailments

It's an unfortunate fact that the human body was not really created to sit on a bicycle. As a result, riding can cause it to suffer in a variety of ways. All common cycling ailments can, however, be alleviated by following a few sensible guidelines. However, you should always seek professional advice from a qualified doctor or sports injury professional if in doubt, especially where a symptom persists or becomes worse despite rest.

Back pain

Cycling, and particularly mountain biking, can hurt your back. However, you can take steps to prevent this. If you suffer from back pain now, go to see a specialist. Physiotherapists, osteopaths and chiropractors can help, but make sure you explain that you're a cyclist, and give them as much information as possible.

If you don't have a bad back, the best prevention is to have your bike set up properly, and to include some stretching as part of each day's activity (see also pp. 82–8). Effective stretching can reduce the likelihood of low back pain occurring. Occasionally sitting upright during rides will help to relieve back strain, as will changing hand positions.

Blisters

Hands and feet are susceptible to blisters and numbness. Wear well-fitting cycle gloves or mitts, comfortable handlebar grips, and set up your bike properly so that you aren't putting too much weight over the front of the bike which will need to be supported by your hands. Most cycle mitts have well-padded palms which relieve pressure and can help to reduce the likelihood of vibration-related pain.

Feet can also suffer during long rides, especially when wet. Make sure shoes fit well; use some Vaseline between the toes and around the heel; and get your feet warm and dry as soon as you can.

Cramps

Cramps are an indication that you are using your muscles beyond their accustomed limit (either for a longer than normal duration, or at a higher than normal level of intensity).

If you are going to be exercising in excessively hot or humid conditions, pay close attention to your fluid and salt intake and add a pinch of salt to your food at these times. A sports drink might help, but maintaining adequate hydration is the key. Finally, if cramps do occur, gently stretching the affected muscle will give relief. Many believe that regular stretching prevents cramps.

Knee pain

Knee pain is the most common cycling-related injury and is completely avoidable in nearly all cases.

To avoid knee pain from the start, get help in setting up your riding position (ask a good shop or very experienced rider), and ride with your feet on the pedals in the position in which they naturally hang – some people's feet point in, some out, and some straight ahead. To check, sit on a table with your feet hanging over the edge, 8 inches apart. Relax. See how your feet point and then set up your pedals and cleats to get your feet in that position when you're on the bike. The ball of the foot should be slightly in front of the pedal axle. Inexperienced riders should limit their pedalling to higher revs – 75–90 per minute – and avoid really steep hills for a few months at least. This will prevent you from using high gears, which put considerable strain on knees.

Treat knee pain with rest, ice (three times a day) and elevate (if swollen) in the first instance. If the knee is still painful after two days see a sports injury specialist. When the pain eventually goes, ease back into training gently. Again, it's best to see a specialist for guidance relating to your particular injury.

Glossary

Aerobic In the presence of oxygen; aerobic metabolism utilises oxygen.

Aerobic power (VO2max) The maximum amount of oxygen that you can extract from the air and utilise in the working muscles for the aerobic production of energy. Also known as aerobic capacity.

Anaerobic Without oxygen; nonoxidation metabolism (see aerobic above).

Body composition Often considered a component of fitness; refers to the makeup of the body in terms of lean mass (muscle, bone, vital tissue and organs) relative to fat mass. An optimal ratio of fat to lean mass is an indication of fitness, and the right type of exercise will help you decrease body fat and increase or maintain muscle mass.

Calorie The commonly used unit of energy, defined as the amount of heat required to increase the temperature of 1 g of water by 1°C.

Cholesterol A form of fat that is ingested in the diet and is also produced in the liver. A high level of cholesterol, and especially a high ratio of total cholesterol to low-density lipoproteins, is associated with increased risk of coronary heart disease.

Conditioning Activities that exercise the whole body to improve overall physical fitness, especially aerobic fitness, musclular strength and endurance, and flexibility.

Cycle ergometer A stationary bike that is calibrated and produces measurable units of work, such that a cyclist's power output can be measured.

Duration The length of time of a given workout.

Endurance The ability of a muscle or group of muscles to overcome a resistance for an extended period of time, and repeatedly. The ability to resist fatigue. Also known as stamina.

Enzymes Complex proteins formed in living cells which assist chemical processes without being changed themselves, i.e. organic catalysts.

Explosive power The ability to develop near-maximal tone in a very short time.

Flexibility The ability to move joints and use muscles through their full range of motion.

Frequency The number of times per week that one trains.

Glucose Simple sugar.

Glycogen The form in which glucose is stored in the muscles and liver.

Hormones Chemical messengers produced by the body and transported in the blood to the target tissue.

Intensity The level of work, or how hard one is working.

Intensity threshold Also called 'onset of blood lactate accumulation (OBLA)', or lactate threshold. The workload at which lactate production is greater than lactate removal; lactate builds up to a level which interferes with muscular contraction.

Interval training Consists of intermittent exercise with regular rest periods. The ratio of work to rest is manipulated according to the desired training effect.

Maximum heart rate The maximum heart rate possible for an individual during any given exercise modality.

Maximum oxygen uptake (VO2max) See aerobic power.

Metabolic rate (metabolism) The rate at which your body burns calories.

Muscular endurance The ability of a muscle or group of muscles to exert force to overcome a resistance, repeatedly and for an extended period of time.

Muscular strength An expression of the amount of force generated by one single, maximum contraction. Refers to the ability of a muscle or group of muscles to exert maximum force to overcome a resistance.

Overload A training load that challenges the body's current level of fitness.

Pain tolerance The ability to continue a high work rate while suffering discomfort in the propulsive muscles.

Power The product of force and velocity, or strength X speed.

Progression Increasing overload at just the right rate to result in fitness gains.

Repetitions Number of times an exercise is repeated.

Sets A group of exercises performed in repetitions and separated by a recovery period.

Specificity A principle of training which dictates that in order to improve a certain component of fitness or in a given activity, a person must train specifically for that component or activity.

Strength The force that a muscle or group of muscles can exert against a resistance.

Taper Reduction in training levels to ensure that an athlete is fresh for a competitive event.

Index

abdominal exercises 71–2
aerobic
    conditioning 109
    exercises 2, 52
    power [VO2] 52, 109
arms
    exercises 67–9
    stretching 88

back
    exercises 73
    pain 107
    stretching 87
bicycles
    choosing 8-12
blood pressure 2
brakes 38

carbohydrates 93–4
chest
    exercises 74
    stretching 88
clothing 20–1
computers, cycle 25
cooling-down 45
crank sets 38–9

dehydration 104–6
descending hills 35–6
diets
    balanced 97–100
    training 101–3

endurance 51–2
exercise
    benefits 2
    cooling-down 45
    upper body 67–74

warming-up 45
exercise bikes 7
explosive power 110
eye protection 24

fat [body] 95
fat [dietary] 96

gears 11
glycogen storage 79, 94

health checks, pre-training 41–3,
heart
    problems 2
    stroke volume 53
heart rate monitors 25
helmets 19–20
hill climbing 34–5
hip muscles, stretching 86
hybrid bikes 9
hydration 91–2, 104–6

interval training 45, 51

knee pain 109

legs, stretching 82–4

massage 89
minerals, dietary 97
mountain bikes 9
mountain biking
    climbs 34–5
    code of conduct 37
    descents 35–6
    obstacles 32–3
    muscles 80–1

pedalling 12–14, 27–8
proteins